WHEN SCRIPTURE MEETS
THE STREETS

When Scripture Meets the Streets

WHAT THE BIBLE SAYS ABOUT EVERYDAY EVENTS

Rev. Van Richmond

Burning Bush Publishing

Foreword

LESSONS FROM THE INTERSECTION OF LIFE
AND THE BIBLE

Our lives are filled with daily lessons. Opportunities to learn, to develop spiritually, to better understand God's intent for how we are to conduct ourselves as His representatives across the face of this globe.

In the midst of the fierce winds of our tornado-paced activities, God speaks through His Holy Word about the situations we find ourselves swirling in. His desire is for us to realize that He has foreseen each and every event – and He has provided perfect guidance to assist us in navigating the intricate and difficult days.

Mark Twain once rightly noted, "A man who carries a cat by the tail learns something he can learn in no other way." My hope and prayer is these stories from life and the related scripture verses will serve as both inspiration and guidance. Perhaps they will enable you to learn the lessons without suffering through the painful scratching and clawing yourself.

The greatest goal is for these lessons from life to demonstrate the love God has for mankind – and for you.

Blessings!

Rev. Van Richmond
Nashville, Tennessee

What People Are Saying About "When Scripture Meets the Streets"

In his newest book, When Scripture Meets the Streets: What the Bible Says About Everyday Events, Van Richmond writes from an expansive ministry experience as a motivational speaker, pastor, educator, and denominational church leader. Richmond is no theorist; proven from more than forty years of practical, successful experience in communicating effectively and motivationally. I am a personal witness to his success and his own ability to communicate with purpose having known him and witnessed his life and ministry for many years. I know that as you read this book you will discover the simple biblical truths that will encourage you and enable you to be an instrument of encouragement to those you meet in everyday life.

Mike Hand, Ph.D.
Tom Elliff Center for Missions
Oklahoma Baptist University
Shawnee, Oklahoma

Pastor Van Richmond is a gifted storyteller. Our brother both inspires and challenges in his recent book, "When Scripture Meets the

Streets: What the Bible Says About Everyday Events". It is a "must read" for the growing Christ follower.

Dr. Neal Hughes
Director of Missions
Montgomery Baptist Association
Montgomery, Alabama

"Many of us if not most of us have heard the saying, "I would rather see a sermon, than hear a sermon". Well that is the purpose of this inspirational, funny, and touching book by my friend Pastor Van Richmond, "When Scripture Meets the Streets: What the Bible Says about Everyday Events". The stories in this book bring Scripture alive and applicable when dealing with events that we all face in life. This book is full of practical illustrations that can be used in any sermon or Bible Study. However the best thing I love about this book is that all of us can relate and see ourselves in many of the stories. Thank you, Pastor Van, for a book that both pastors and members will be blessed by."

Fred Luter, Jr.
Pastor, Franklin Avenue Baptist Church
New Orleans, LA.
Former President, Southern Baptist Convention

No one on earth has stories to tell like the man that has given his life to the call of God to pastor. One such pastor has taken the time to tell those stories in WHEN SCRIPTURE MEETS THE STREETS. It is real, honest, surprising, and fun to read. Pastor Van Richmond has taken big doses of humor, encouragement, and Godly perspective to bless us readers of his excellent work.

Randy C. Davis
President & Executive Director
Tennessee Baptist Mission Board

Thank you Van! What a refreshing compendium of real life accounts touching virtually every emotion. Refreshing reminders of our humanity, God's sovereignty and Christ's amazing grace. Like delicacies on a plate, it's hard to savor just one! Bless you for using your "front row seat" in life's arena to remind us all that our lives are both serious and sometimes just plain silly. Bless you for taking time to tell us these touching stories.

Dr. Tom Elliff
Former President, Southern Baptist Convention

I love stories of how God has worked in people's lives. Van has captured so many amazing stories of just that. Through these short stories and the scripture that accompanies them, you can celebrate what God is doing each day through your devotional time.

Connie Dixon
President
Woman's Missionary Union (WMU)
Southern Baptist Convention

I have known Van Richmond for more than two decades. He has a passion for preaching the Word of God, but God also gave him the ability to communicate through the written word. His book, "When Scripture Meets the Streets: What the Bible Says About Everyday Events" combines truth from the Bible with funny anecdotes that one can only learn by being a pastor or talking to numerous pastors over the years. The stories he shares will make you both laugh and cry. They are woven together with the ultimate truth that God is in charge of our lives.

Lonnie Wilkey
Editor, *Baptist & Reflector*
Tennessee Baptist Mission Board

Van has an ability to tell an interesting story that helps us remember the point of the Bible verse he is writing about. It's a book you will enjoy!

Jayne Kuryluk
Executive Director
Christian Meetings and Convention Association

1

Easily Distracted by Shiny Objects

Proverbs 4:25 (NCV) - Keep your eyes focused on what is right, and look straight ahead to what is good.

The phrase "Easily distracted by shiny objects" describes most people rather accurately, though the shiny objects will vary for each person. In actuality, the object doesn't even have to be shiny to divert our attention. A bigger house. A less difficult job assignment. A hobby or collection that dominates our focus. Getting sidetracked happens pretty easily since we learned that skill at an early age.

Bobbi Greene is a Nashville-area teacher, and she posted on Facebook a wonderful example of the challenge you and I face. (First she gave the situation and then she related the dialogue.) "Conversation today with a first grader who is very smart and capable of finishing work but is getting a little lazy here at the end of the year. I'm making her look at me and being very serious:

Mrs. Greene. – "Now tomorrow, you really need to get your work done. You need to be ready for 2nd grade, and finishing your work is part of that. You need to stay focused and get busy."

1st Grader – "I like your dress."

The ability to "stay focused and get busy" applies as we go about accomplishing school work, housework, professional work, and God's work. The challenge is difficult because there are just SO MANY shiny objects! Former President George W. Bush noted, "I would like to be remembered as a guy who had a set of priorities and was willing to live by those priorities."

The glint of the shiny object, though, is mesmerizing. Priorities get pushed aside. God's work goes unattended in favor of the unimportant. Romans 8:5 (ESV) summarized this concept well in saying "For those who live according to the flesh set their minds on the things of the flesh, but those who live according to the Spirit set their minds on the things of the Spirit."

To paraphrase Mrs. G, living according to the Spirit requires "Finishing our work." It really comes down to this: getting distracted by shiny objects is much harder when your priority is making your life shine for Jesus. Get focused – "Look straight ahead to what is good."

My most significant takeaways:

How I will apply this:

Other related scriptures:

2

When Attacks Come

March 5, 1999, was just another ordinary day at the offices of the Southern Baptist Convention's Executive Committee. The routine atmosphere of lunchtime darkened instantly when the receptionist entered my wife's office and said, "I don't know what to do about this," as she handed Lynn an envelope. My wife pulled out a card that read, "Congratulations, you have just been exposed to anthrax."

Emergency procedures were implemented. The building was locked down. Air handlers were shut off. Officials swarmed the scene as the FBI was joined by personnel from the Metro Nashville Health Department, the Office of Emergency Management, and the Police and Fire Departments.

Countless prayers and the professional handling of the situation by emergency personnel served to lessen the anxieties of the four staff members who had come into contact with the card. Since they had possibly been exposed to deadly anthrax bacteria, protocol dictated a bleach and water decontamination shower and scrub-brushing, followed by a month of heavy-duty antibiotics. Hardly a routine or ordinary day.

Attacks leave us feeling as though we inhaled spores of hatred. Vile comments lock down our heart and shut off our air supply. Anonymous slander triggers an emergency response. When David faced violent, lying, evil men, he made a 911 call to his righteous defender. He began with a daily fortification: "Each morning I will look to you in heaven and lay my requests before you, praying earnestly." Psalm 5:3 (TLB)

Verse six demonstrates his assurance in God – "You will destroy them for their lies; how you abhor all murder and deception." In fact, David asks the Lord to share this confidence-building remedy with every believer who faces unprovoked and undeserved attacks: "Make everyone rejoice who puts his trust in you. Keep them shouting for joy because you are defending them."

Those few hours on March 5 were unlike any before or since for our family. While we fought with prayer as our sole weapon, the battle truly was God's. We knew the outcome would ultimately be wonderful, regardless of how that particular day and particular event turned out: "For you bless the godly man, O Lord; you protect him with your shield of love." (verse 12)

My most significant takeaways:

How I will apply this:

Other related scriptures:

3

'Cause You've Got Personality

She walked through the door and immediately launched into a high-speed, non-stop monologue that left me feeling like I had just undergone five minutes in a gale-force wind tunnel. Her impromptu speech torrent went something like, "Hi, my nickname is Bulldog, and I've got two dogs, I've got a 35-pound Boston bulldog and this AKC-registered Maltese that my ex-husband brought in, and I really don't need two dogs...would you like to have the Maltese because the bulldog and I have the same kind of personality and I really don't need the extra dog because I work so many hours, so would you like to take the Maltese?"

Who knew it was possible to experience a verbal hurricane? Once this dynamo of discourse blew out of the training room where I was working, her words began to slowly drop from the still-swirling air currents. Meeting a woman with such a distinctive nickname was unique enough, but I was especially intrigued by her psychological assessment of the similarities in personality between her and her loveable, mug-ugly bulldog.

In a serious self-evaluation, with whom (or even with what) would you say your personality aligns? The second question would ask: are you truly happy with the close parallel between yourself and that person

11

(or pup). Whom would you prefer to be like? Some television or movie celebrity? A sports star? Your favorite teacher? A caring neighbor?

The best answer for followers of Jesus lies in the words of the apostle Paul, who said, "Therefore be imitators of God, as beloved children. And walk in love, as Christ loved us and gave himself up for us, a fragrant offering and sacrifice to God." (Ephesians 5:1-2 ESV)

Children often want to be like their father or mother. Being an imitator of our heavenly Father leads us to examine our behaviors to see how they align, to see if our "personalities" are alike. After all, God sets a rather high standard when it comes to goodness, grace, mercy, and justice.

Maybe you just need to approach the challenge of imitating God with the tenacity of a bulldog. If you sink your teeth into the wonderful opportunity to walk in love every day, your efforts and the ensuing results will a delightful offering to God. You can do it, as Lloyd Price sang, "'Cause you've got personality!"

You have the personality of God.

My most significant takeaways:

How I will apply this:

Other related scriptures:

4

Being Upfront About Being Up Front

When Major Lee Chaffin oversaw the SWAT team, he was assigned a new drug-detecting dog. Duke was an obedient partner that was easy to work with, and he thoroughly enjoyed riding in the front seat of Lee's patrol vehicle. Unfortunately, testing and training revealed that that Duke would rather sniff for food than sniff out drugs, so he had to leave law enforcement.

Lee's father was delighted to take Duke, but another challenge soon surfaced. His new canine chum was accustomed to being up front and refused any other spot. As a result, Lee's mother was forced to ride in the back seat, creating a picture reminiscent of the movie, "Driving Miss Daisy."

Sometimes people can feel like Duke did. They want to be up front in a position of prominence. Taking a back seat to others? Not their style. They would rather be center stage than be a stagehand. Rather lead the parade than build the float. Solomon offered guidance that makes the Dukes of the world uncomfortable but serves Christians well. In Proverbs 29:23 (ESV), the wise king wrote, "One's pride will bring him low, but he who is lowly in spirit will obtain honor."

An old man lost 40-50 per cent of his blood volume when he was severely injured. While he was hospitalized for recuperation, a friend came to check on him. The visitor heard a voice from the bathroom say, "George, I'm in here. Come on in." There was a natural hesitation before he peered in and saw the old man on his hands and knees, wiping the floor with paper towels. "What are you...doing?" was George's perplexed question. The man replied, "Well, you see, I spilled some water and I don't want the nurses to have to wipe it up."

His reaction was clearly instinctual. It revealed a kind and selfless disposition. The act was also a truly humble one. The man on the floor was President Ronald Reagan following the attempted assassination on his life, and his visitor was Vice President George H. Bush. Even though elderly and in poor health, this most powerful man felt no self-importance. Mr. Reagan made the spill, so he swabbed the floor.

"Do nothing from rivalry or conceit, but in humility count others more significant than yourselves." (Philippians 2:3 ESV) Be willing to take a back seat in life and in ministry. You may discover the view is grander than you ever imagined.

My most significant takeaways:

How I will apply this:

Other related scriptures:

5

Scarred For Life

We stepped off the bus in downtown Frankfurt, Germany, in April of 1980. Our Air Force temporary duty assignment to Rhein-Main Air Force Base allowed only a brief opportunity for sightseeing, and it was an exciting excursion for this country boy from northeastern Kentucky. The initial impression of Frankfurt's similarity to any number of mid-sized American cities faded within moments. Bullet holes of varying sizes dotted the facades of numerous buildings, stark reminders of the WWII battles that had raged there less than forty years earlier.

Nineteen years later and more than 7,300 miles westward, my family and I toured Hickam Air Force Base in Honolulu, Hawaii. Multiple bullet holes in the Headquarters building and the base hospital grimly spoke of the WWII attack on December 7, 1941, referred to by President Franklin D. Roosevelt as "a date which will live in infamy." Those scars of war are reminders to never be unprepared.

Most people carry scars. Surgeries, accidents, or someone else's actions can leave visible scars. Other wounds can't be seen. Emotional bullet holes can remain in our psyches decades after the painful event. If we are not careful, a dangerous infection can set up in our psychological wound and spread throughout our body with devastating results. The physical marks cannot always be remedied, but our Great Physician gives directions on combatting the internal wounds. Ephesians 4:31-32

(ESV) tells us, "Let all bitterness and wrath and anger and clamor and slander be put away from you, along with all malice. Be kind to one another, tenderhearted, forgiving one another, as God in Christ forgave you."

Be kind, tenderhearted, forgiving. Painful history does not force us to inflict pain upon others. Our scars are not to dictate our actions. Pastor Edwin Hubbell Chapin saw value in the marks, and his perspective is well worth considering: "Out of suffering have emerged the strongest souls; the most massive characters are seamed with scars; martyrs have put on their coronation robes glittering with fire, and through their tears have the sorrowful first seen the gates of heaven."

Everyone, in some way, has been scarred for life, just like the walls of Frankfurt and Hickam. The most important mark you carry, though, the one that defines your very existence and purpose, is the impression of the cross of Christ on your heart.

My most significant takeaways:

How I will apply this:

Other related scriptures:

6

How Big Is Your Heart?

The word "heart" has been used to describe the real but immeasurable trait that defines both highly successful people and animals, such as thoroughbred horses. "Heart" captures the will to win, the temperament to give everything possible, and it is frequently used when experts refer to 1973 Triple Crown-winner Secretariat. He still holds the records in the Kentucky Derby, the Preakness, and the Belmont races. During the autopsy following the death of the big chestnut colt, pathologist Dr. Thomas Swerczek said he and his colleagues stopped and stood in stunned silence. The heart of an average horse weighs eight and one-half pounds; the team estimated the weight of Secretariat's heart at twenty-two pounds. With his big heart, this magnificent athlete accomplished things other horses couldn't.

For people, the physical size of their heart is not a determining factor in their daily lives. However, people who have a big "heart" accomplish things other people do not, simply because they have a different mindset. Matthew 6:21 helps us understand what is truly important in our lives when it says, "For where your treasure is, there your heart will be also." Now, what do you deeply treasure?

The Grinch, Dr. Seuss' famed character, had a heart that was two sizes too small. Such is not the case for the owners of the Double Comfort restaurant in Columbus, Ohio. This company's noteworthy mission demonstrates their treasure: people in need. For each meal purchased, a meal is donated to the local food bank. Comfort for the patron, comfort for someone less fortunate. Jesus taught his disciples this principle when He said, "Do not store up for yourselves treasures on earth, where moths and vermin destroy, and where thieves break in and steal. But store up for yourselves treasures in heaven." (Matthew 6:19-20 NIV)

Secretariat was featured on the cover of Sports Illustrated, Time, and Newsweek in the same week, an accomplishment that has never been repeated. There were so many demands for public appearances that his owners hired the William Morris Agency, making him probably the only horse with a Hollywood agent. The U.S. Postal Service even issued a commemorative stamp in his honor.

Great rewards do come to those who have big hearts.

My most significant takeaways:

How I will apply this:

Other related scriptures:

7

Walking Tall

Busy. People are so busy today. And focused, too. When they decide to fully concentrate, nothing or no one will divert their single-mindedness. Such was the case as the gentleman walked hurriedly through the concourse of the convention center during the 2015 Southern Baptist Convention Pastors' Conference. He was busy, engrossed in reading and sending texts. Hundreds of people around him. Vendors' booths lining both sides of the aisle. Nothing could break his focus – until he walked headfirst into a steel column and knocked himself out cold!

We are not radar-equipped. No bat sensors to alert us of impending dangers. Walking blindly can be hazardous to your health, but seeing walkers engrossed in their phone instead of their surroundings has become the norm. This oft-repeated act brings to mind the rabbit in the scene from the classic movie, *Alice in Wonderland,* where the harried hare checks his clock and scurries away while saying,

"I'm late, I'm late,

for a very important date.

No time to say hello, good-bye,

I'm late, I'm late, I'm late."

What a perfect descriptor of modern life. Rushing, but to where? To accomplish what? Are the "very important dates" truly that important?

God has a different path, one that will not require treatment by paramedics. Ephesians 5:15-16 (ESV) offers, "Look carefully then how you walk, not as unwise but as wise, making the best use of the time, because the days are evil." He wants us to be aware of the evil obstacles, the barriers that can knock us out of effective service to Him.

Slow down. Wise up. A lady laughed while telling about her boat tour through the San Antonio Riverwalk. She watched in disbelief as a woman on the sidewalk became so engrossed in texting that she stepped off the pavement and splashed face-first into the San Antonio River.

Hopefully it won't take a bruised head or bruised pride to get us to lift our eyes. The days are evil, so minister to and love others. Tell them about Jesus. Those activities truly are the best use of our time.

My most significant takeaways:

How I will apply this:

Other related scriptures:

8

Nothing but the Truth

Texas school superintendent Barbara Marchbanks told about her grandson, Andrew, who views the world through a prism of either black or white. Gray is nonexistent. His narrow focus and forthright manner initiated an event at summer school that sent teachers and faculty members running from the anticipated human eruption.

Andrew was seated at lunch beside a teacher who is known to have the personality of a rattlesnake. He apparently saw her as being physically large – very, very large. Speaking with all the truth as seen from his seven years of living, he bluntly asked, "Have you ever tried working out or exercising?" Utter silence swept over the room as seconds ticked by. She turned to the lad and slowly replied, "No." While still working on his lunch, Andrew answered, "Well, maybe you should." The teacher once more paused for several moments before answering, "Well, maybe I will."

Truth. Not always welcome. Teachers now tell Barbara they are definitely not going to sit beside Andrew. Truth sometimes stands outside our door accompanied by its friends, Discomfort and Pain. In the movie, *A Few Good Men,* Jack Nicholson immortalized the phrase, "You can't handle the truth!" It seems many people today can't handle the truth of God's existence. Can't handle the truth of Jesus as the single path to heaven. Can't handle the truth contained in scripture. But why? 1 Corinthians 2:14 (NCV) answers: "A person who does not have the Spirit does not accept the truths that come from the Spirit of God."

Remember the oath taken by witnesses: "Do you swear to tell the truth, the whole truth, and nothing but the truth?" Telling the truth, and nothing but the truth, is our tasking. Help for those without the Spirit is available it we are available. We are directed by 1 John 3:18 (ESV) to "not love in word or talk but in deed and in truth." Your close friends, Truth and Love, can open the hardest doors and allow the Spirit to enter the heart of someone who previously couldn't handle truth.

Bold Christians can shake the world by telling the truth. Little Andrew's boldness shook the cafeteria. Find someone and tell them they should work out – their life, their struggles, and their eternity – with Jesus.

My most significant takeaways:

How I will apply this:

Other related scriptures:

9

Have It Your Way

Tractor trailer rigs and people are sometimes alike. Either can get out of control. Travel along mountain interstate highways and you will see the runaway truck ramps on the downward slopes. Wide lanes cut upward into the mountain are filled with loose gravel. These escape routes serve to quickly halt a heavily-loaded 18-wheeler that has lost its brakes. Lives have been saved. Injuries avoided. Trucks and their cargo are preserved. What do you do, though, with a person who is out of control? Does anyone build runaway ramps for people?

"Alicia" showed up unannounced one Saturday afternoon as Lynn and I were in the middle of the week's laundry. Glad to see her, we were most pleasantly surprised when Alicia offered to help fold the freshly-washed towels and sheets. (She could come every Saturday if she wants!)

We folded towels in a particular way so they fit more compactly in the closet. Alicia folded our towels her way, but that didn't matter to us. It was folding towels, not thoracic spinal surgery. Folded is folded, right? Alicia grabbed the basket of linens, and as she opened the closet door, she softly murmured, "Oh, no." We laughed as we watched the transformation. Alicia became the out-of-control runaway truck barreling down the crooked mountain road. Her OCD nature pushed the accelerator and cut the brake lines. Her way became the only way

23

as she carefully, methodically removed and refolded every single item. Her way.

"Have it your way." The burger chain's advertising slogan has become the world's guide to living. Take down the guard rails. Ignore the speed limits. Live life to the fullest. Have it your way. The sales pitch is enticing, but the consequences are dire. To protect us, the Lord created a runaway ramp. In 1 Corinthians 10:13, Paul says, "No temptation has overtaken you that is not common to man. God is faithful, and he will not let you be tempted beyond your ability, but with the temptation he will also provide the way of escape, that you may be able to endure it."

Be like Alicia. Be like the hamburger chain. Have it your way. Of course, you will rapidly discover your way is the best way – when it aligns with God's way.

My most significant takeaways:

How I will apply this:

Other related scriptures:

10

Are You a Heart Donor Candidate?

We didn't expect to be in the Vanderbilt Hospital emergency room in the wee hours of the morning. The chest pains that jolted me awake just after midnight, combined with my family history of heart disease, led us to this unexpected situation and location. Two hours and a battery of tests later, the doctors felt reasonably sure I had not experienced a heart attack, but they wanted to conduct one final assessment – a treadmill stress test.

When I totally surpassed the standards on the stress test, the surprised radiology doctor commented, "You have a good heart." The results were forwarded to the ER physician, who confidently dismissed me from the hospital by saying, "You've got one of the best hearts here!" What comforting, reassuring words! My heart is strong; it's physically good enough to donate for a transplant.

Consider this question: If God were examining you to determine if your heart was fit to be transplanted, what would He discover?

When the Great Physician opened your body, would he find your heart "is in the right place," or would He be searching in vain because you had "lost heart?" Would the Creator describe you as having "the heart of a leader" or "the heart of a lion?" Did you have a light heart or a heavy heart?

Would He discover your heart is filled with joy, or would the chambers be clogged with anger? Did you have a heart of gold or a heart of stone? Could it be you had a diseased heart - were you sick at heart, or maybe had a broken heart?

Was your heart worn out from pumping joy into the world or rusted out from disuse? What about the navigation system in your heart – were you a person after God's own heart, or did it lead you to follow along after the world?

In Jeremiah 17:10 we read, "I the Lord search the heart and examine the mind, to reward each person according to their conduct, according to what their deeds deserve."

To be a heart donor candidate, your heart must be good. Let me encourage you to renew your heartfelt commitment to the one who died for your sins, and then allow God to direct your steps and your service.

When you live for Him, it will do your heart good.

My most significant takeaways:

How I will apply this:

Other related scriptures:

11

Be a Mover and a Shaker

My wife and I were walking on the campus of Berry College in Rome, Georgia, heading toward the old grist mill. As we casually made our way along the half-mile gravel road, simply strolling and enjoying the delightfully cool August evening, we noticed a rather unusual phenomenon in the trees ahead.

The branches from two different types of trees were intertwined, as frequently happens in a heavily timbered area, and as a result, leaves from each tree were jutting into the territory of surrounding trees. Oddly, the gentle breeze we enjoyed at ground level produced a strange result as it moved through the boughs.

The leaves of one tree were dancing about at a frantic pace, moving and shaking in something akin to a forested Foxtrot. A cluster of leaves from the second, intertwined tree was literally beside the leaves from the first tree, yet there was scarcely any movement to be detected, looking more like a junior-high slow dance.

It seems Christians are often much like those tree leaves. When one feels the Spirit moving, they respond immediately with visible and productive activity. The second, if they stir at all, moves slowly and slightly. Thankfully, Jesus gave us the guide for a desirable response in Luke 22:27 (NASB) when he said, "For who is greater, the one who reclines at the table or the one who serves? Is it not the one who reclines at the table? But I am among you as the one who serves."

When the Spirit moves in our life, our response should be to stop reclining and start helping. Responding means you begin to move, to share, to serve. Conversely, rebelling against the Spirit and rigidly battling any movement does nothing to aid in the battle for lost souls.

God doesn't lead us to simply show up on Sunday, enjoy the worship, and go home merely to repeat the process the next week. We are called to serve. Whether teaching a class, calling to encourage and pray for someone, or taking responsibility for one of the many other available and necessary ministries, the Holy Spirit calls each of us.

The Spirit doesn't call us to merely hang around, being unproductive or rigidly resistant. When the Spirit speaks, let others see your visible movement as you go about God's work. Be tenacious, turned on, and turned loose.

Be a mover and a shaker.

My most significant takeaways:

How I will apply this:

Other related scriptures:

12

Being Thankful For the Gift of Memory

During the holidays of Thanksgiving, Christmas, and New Year's Day, occasions abound when we can pause and be thankful for the varied and many gifts we have been blessed with. Our finest gifts are often things that cannot be purchased, including the gift of memory.

Memory allows us to become time travelers, mentally hopping back and forth between decades and events in a mere instant, jetting from the Junior High prom to the birth of your first child to wading through floodwaters as you helped rescue stranded neighbors.

Because of the gift of memory, we can once again hear our Mother's laughter. See the undersized, Charlie Brown-style Christmas tree you had the first year of marriage. Smell the tantalizing aroma of Grandma's luscious apple pie as it came out of the oven. Family trips; the first time to see the ocean; the day of the funeral – those undying memories stir different emotions within us, bringing a fresh wave of joy, a fleeting smile, or possibly even a few tears.

Keith Boyd shared that his uncle, who had battled leukemia, left a sizeable portion of his estate to St. Jude's Hospital upon his death. Keith observed that when the family gathers on Thanksgiving, the memories that surface always include their deceased uncle. But following his uncle's passing, the family has chosen to not merely relive old memories but to create new ones.

In the years following his uncle's death, as many as 30 family members have gathered and participated in the St. Jude's Marathon. Some of their clan take part in the one-mile Family Fun Run; Keith runs the half-marathon while his mother determinedly walks the same 13.1 miles. What great memories to discuss in the future – painful blisters, achy muscles, and the warm satisfaction of knowing they contributed to such a worthy cause as St. Jude's Hospital.

The apostle Paul wrote to the church of Philippi, saying, "I thank my God in all my remembrance of you." (Philippians 1:3) Memory gives us the unmatched privilege of enjoying remembrances of beloved family members, God's saints, true friends, and special occasions.

Memories might be vivid or faded, joyful or painful, accurately captured or embellished by time, but they are ours. As your memory time machine transports you back and forth during the holidays, enjoy your memories fully, even those that might harbor a tinge of sadness. Be grateful for the gift of memory, and look for the opportunities to create new, lasting memories to add to your mental video collection.

It will provide years of delightful future viewing.

My most significant takeaways:

How I will apply this:

Other related scriptures:

13

I Am Blessed

His baseball cap said everything.

"I Am Blessed"

The elderly gentleman's dark maroon hat spoke his message loudly as it proclaimed his thankful perspective on life. Apparently being in a medical rehab facility wasn't dampening his spirits. The twinkle in his eye was a beacon that drew you in. What some might call wrinkles on his face were actually laugh lines produced by decades of sharing his optimistic outlook.

Perhaps he saw his mode of transportation – a powered wheelchair – as a means to perform daredevil stunts. Racing through the dining room awakened a long-forgotten sense of excitement in the hearts of other residents as he zoomed precariously close to their limp salads or dull desserts.

Having a prosthetic right leg did not concern this supercharged senior citizen. It simply meant his days of acquiring new skills were continuing. Apparently he never bought into the "You can't teach an old dog new tricks" mantra. Keeping your body active helps keep your mind active, so he was receiving a double benefit.

Maybe this gentleman actually read and believed Romans 8:28 - "And we know that God causes everything to work together for the good of those who love God and are called according to his purpose for them" (NLT).

Lord, your plan is perfect; our plans lean toward preposterous. We can whine when difficulties come, or we can whisper our gratitude that you are working for our good. Today, Father, whether you choose to give or to take away, only one response is truly appropriate:

I am blessed.

My most significant takeaways:

How I will apply this:

Other related scriptures:

14

A Taste For Something More

New environments can offer exciting new opportunities. The move in 1965 for Lowry and Charlotte Allen suggested a very different culture and lifestyle lay ahead. For a young man from Kentucky and a Mississippi-born Southern Belle, relocating from Bowling Green, Kentucky, to Houston, Texas, presented a distinctly different environment. Bowling Green had no ethnic cafes such as Mexican restaurants or pizza parlors at that time, so Charlotte's taste buds went on hyper alert when she began spotting Hispanic eateries in their new home city.

After some pleading and cajoling one evening, she convinced the rather reluctant Lowry to take her to dinner at a nearby Mexican restaurant. Oh, the anticipation! Charlotte scanned the menu, searching for the perfect meal for her introductory journey into a previously undiscovered culinary world. She could hardly wait! Lowry, on the other hand, simply ordered a grilled cheese sandwich.

Isn't that often the way people are when God takes them somewhere new? It doesn't matter whether it is a new physical location or a new area of ministry. People are often reluctant to try something new. We just sing again and again the oldies line from Frankie Valli and the Four Seasons, "Let's hang on, to what we've got."

Holding on to what we've got (the past) prohibits us from embracing the wonderful future the Lord has for us and those He brings us into contact with. Let's do our best to make God's ways our ways.

In Philippians 3:12-14 (The Message), we find superb guidance on how to accomplish that: "I'm not saying that I have this all together, that I have it made. But I am well on my way, reaching out for Christ, who has so wondrously reached out for me. Friends, don't get me wrong: By no means do I count myself an expert in all of this, but I've got my eye on the goal, where God is beckoning us onward—to Jesus. I'm off and running, and I'm not turning back."

Instead of telling our Father, "Grilled cheese for me!" let's swallow our fears and try a taste of something more. After all, if Christ had been concerned with His personal comfort, He would have stayed in heaven. You probably will never be asked to hang on a cross for mankind, but we are asked to not hang out with the comfortable past.

It comes down to trusting God. Instead of singing, "Let's hang on," try learning a new song. Go with the Hank Snow country music classic, "I'm Movin' On!"

My most significant takeaways:

How I will apply this:

Other related scriptures:

15

Seeing Your Situation Differently

Struggles. Everyone faces them. Financial, relational, employment, health – whatever your particular malady might involve, it can often consume you, dominating every waking moment (and even some when you are asleep). Pastor and author Max Lucado helps us see our situation differently with this wonderful story.

Defiant Joy
by Max Lucado

My friend Rob cried freely telling his story about his young son's challenging life.

Daniel was born with a double cleft palate, dramatically disfiguring his face. He had surgery, but the evidence remains, so people constantly notice and occasionally make remarks.

Daniel, however, is unfazed! He just tells people God made him this way so, what's the big deal? He was named student of the week, so he was asked to bring something to show his classmates for show and tell. Daniel told his mom he wanted to take the pictures that showed his face prior to the surgery. His mom was concerned. "Won't that make you feel a bit funny?" she asked. But Daniel insisted, "Oh, no, I want everyone to see what God did for me!"

Try Daniel's defiant joy and see what happens. God has handed you a cup of blessings. Sweeten it with a heaping spoonful of gratitude!

When the quicksand of your situation threatens to suck you in, view it with gratitude as Daniel did, and remember the encouraging words of Isaiah 41:10 – Do not fear, for I am with you; do not be afraid, for I am your God. I will strengthen you; I will help you; I will hold on to you with My righteous right hand.

My most significant takeaways:

How I will apply this:

Other related scriptures:

16

Stop Right There!

Our grandson, Brayden, was playing in a baseball league for four- and five-year-olds. He was playing second base, and when an opponent was running from first base toward second, Brayden extended his hand like a traffic cop and authoritatively exclaimed, "Stop right there!" The befuddled player did just that, halting midway between bases and looking quizzically back to his coach on first.

Wouldn't life be wonderful if you could hit the pause button on those pesky negatives by simply commanding, "Stop right there!" The interfering in-law, the ache in your body, or the hurt in your heart – each stopped dead in its tracks by three little words. Disease could be brought to a standstill. Traffic would wait for you to pass. The bank foreclosure would be forgotten about – all because of one emphatic utterance. How sweet life would be!

Admittedly, people are averse to adversity, but could there possibly be any value in facing challenges? Billy Graham observed, "Comfort and prosperity have never enriched the world as much as adversity has." Right now, you may have just assessed your life, felt like it was enriched way too much by adversity, and decided you don't like Billy Graham anymore. How could he possibly say such a thing? The Bible helps us better understand his assertion with a single verse: "Friends love through all kinds of weather." Proverbs 17:17 (The Message)

Painful though it is, adversity lets you determine who your fair-weather friends are. Renowned Bible scholar Matthew Henry refers to "swallow-friends" that fly to you in summer but are gone in winter. John 13:1 describes how Jesus loved his companions to the end. We personally see an uplifting Christ-likeness in our friends who don't disappear when storm clouds darken our horizon.

True friends are a gift from heaven, and we thoroughly enjoy the relationship we share with them. A 95-year-old spinster in a nursing home confided to a fellow church member that she was worried sick. When the church member asked what was troubling her, the lady leaned back in her rocking chair, sighed a heavy sigh, then slowly explained her major worry. "Every close friend I ever had has already died and gone on to heaven. I'm afraid they're all wondering where I went."

The next time challenges abound and you are tempted to declare "Stop right there!", well…, just stop right there. Instead, offer thanks to God for how He is enriching your world with adversity and for the true friends who stride alongside as you trudge through the storms.

My most significant takeaways:

How I will apply this:

Other related scriptures:

17

Sweet!

A single word can conjure up many different visions, and "sweet" could readily be the best to describe our worship gathering on July 7, 2013.

Recall your fondest memories from a family, high school, or college reunion, and you have a delightful mental taste of the sweet fellowship at New Life Church.

Dr. Jerry Sutton returned to Nashville to preach for the New Life Church family, and a record attendance of 116 blessed us by joining in the worship service. It was exciting to see cherished friends and familiar acquaintances from a bygone time as they reunited, even if for just a brief period, to hear God's word preached by a dear friend. The expressions of sheer delight that crossed visitors' faces, accompanied by many, many hugs and hearty handshakes, stirred remembrances from days gone by when all of us were in a very different part of our life, career, and ministry.

I can't help but think that that experience was just a tiny sliver of the boundless joy and celebration we will feel upon entering the gates of heaven. Colossians 3: 4 says, "When Christ, who is your life, appears, then you also will appear with him in glory." Add this appealing aspect shared by Luke: "People will come from east and west and north and south, and will take their places at the feast in the kingdom of God.

Indeed there are those who are last who will be first, and first who will be last." (Luke 13:29-30)

The Apostle John writes from his island of exile, saying, "He will wipe every tear from their eyes. There will be no more death or mourning or crying or pain, for the old order of things has passed away." He who was seated on the throne said, "I am making everything new!" (Rev. 21:4 NIV)

We will appear with Christ in glory, partaking of the feast in the kingdom of God as we mark the end of death, mourning, crying, and pain. Our joy will reach unparalleled levels as we delight in the most amazing reunion possible.

What will it be like when we finally reach home?

Sweet!

My most significant takeaways:

How I will apply this:

Other related scriptures:

18

The Hunger for Love

Tammy Garvin is our great friend and the woman who attempts to make my unruly hair look somewhat presentable. One of her clients and her three daughters were in Tammy's salon, and the three girls soon became the center of attention for the whole room.

A waiting patron asked took an interest in the children and asked the oldest girl, "What do you want to be when you grow up?" "A teacher," came the quick and confident answer. When the same question was posed to the second daughter, she twirled around the room and gaily replied, "I'm going to be a dancer."

Now it was the bright-eyed three-year old's turn, and when queried about her future plans, she offered an immediate but puzzling response: "I want to be a biscuit."

In a scene reminiscent of the E.F. Hutton commercials from years ago, everything in the salon went totally silent as all eyes turned toward Little Miss. The grandmotherly-type who had been engaging the three young ladies then posed a follow-up question that clearly indicated her confusion: "Why do you want to be a biscuit?"

The captivating youngster sweetly whispered, "Because everybody loves biscuits."

Love. How desperately people (including little girls) crave it. Mother Teresa sagely observed, "The hunger for love is much more difficult to remove than the hunger for bread." Like countless people around the globe, the little girl in the salon simply wants to have her hunger for love satisfied.

In John 6:35, Jesus declares, "I am the bread of life. No one who comes to Me will ever be hungry."

Let's do our part to defeat the world's hunger by sharing Jesus with young and old children alike. His satisfying, totally attainable, enduring, life-changing love. And when we do, they will make a great discovery.

The Bread of Life is much better than biscuits.

My most significant takeaways:

How I will apply this:

Other related scriptures:

19

The Yardstick of Life

After meeting with the family so I could prepare for a funeral service, the similarity between that situation and my previous time of employment as a carpenter became readily apparent. Perhaps the most important tools a carpenter possesses are measuring instruments: rulers, tape measures, and even lasers in today's digital world. Without accurate tools for measuring, doors don't fit cabinets, bridges do not align with the incoming highway, or building foundations are smaller than the blueprint's specifications. Accurate measurement is critical.

In life, what is the yardstick that measures the success, the impact, the significance of someone's brief time before their name is carved on a tombstone? As a yardstick is made up of three feet, I believe we can use three factors as the yardstick to measure our steps through life: Family, Fun, and Faith.

Surviving family members repeatedly spoke of the ongoing sense of family this lady created and fostered throughout her life. Everyone felt warm and welcomed at MamMaw's house, with great love and mouth-watering home-cooked meals being showered upon guests, casual acquaintances, and even total strangers who crossed the threshold of her home.

Fun was also a significant part of this lady's existence as she displayed an exciting zest for life. Whether traveling with her husband to

London and seeing the changing of the guard at Buckingham Palace, golfing trips to Myrtle Beach, or participating as a long-time member of the ladies' bowling league, she incorporated a healthy dose of fun into life.

Thankfully, most important to MamMaw was her faith. She had been a Christian for decades, serving and worshiping her Lord and Savior. While she loved her family, she also knew that loving Jesus was more important. In Matthew 10:37, Jesus told his twelve disciples, "The person who loves father or mother more than Me is not worthy of Me; the person who loves son or daughter more than Me is not worthy of Me." This sweet lady understood and embraced that God was to be of greater importance to her than her beloved family.

At some point, God will lay a yardstick beside each of our lives, and He will assess our days and our priorities. Will He discover that you displayed love for your family and for adding to God's family? Will His unerring measurement reflect how much fun you had while reaching out to serve others on His behalf? Most importantly, will your Creator calculate your faith and find you worthy of Him?

My most significant takeaways:

How I will apply this:

Other related scriptures:

20

'Tis the Season of Giving

Snowflakes gently cover the landscape of the small town, silently draping a frosty blanket over the shoulders of lighthearted shoppers. These merry souls eagerly brave the elements and the chilly air as they search out the perfect gift for each person on their Christmas list.

This storybook scenario - and the retailers - cheerily tells us that the most wonderful time of the year has arrived: 'Tis the season of giving.

The challenging part of that phrase is the word "season." We understand the seasons of spring summer, fall, and winter since they are on the calendar. We get deer-hunting season and football season and baseball season. Each has a specified beginning and ending date. But is giving something that is scheduled for 30 days at the end of the year?

Jesus both taught and demonstrated that giving is a year-round process. Without suggesting a season, He instructed the rich young ruler, "Sell all you have and give the money to the poor" (Luke 18:22 ESV).

Then the Messiah showed us how to give. Jesus gift-wrapped comfort and caring to personally deliver to Jews and Gentiles alike. He continually gave thanks to His father and gave the special gift of time to His followers. He gave new life to Lazarus, and He gave his own life for us on what was truly Black Friday.

A true spirit of giving is not triggered by storybook Christmas scenes, snowflakes, and decorated trees. Giving is a mindset that is spurred by the heart, regardless of where the calendar is turned. Psalm 112:6, 9 tells us "For the righteous will never be moved; he will be re-membered forever. He has distributed freely; he has given to the poor; his righteousness endures forever; his horn is exalted in honor."

Dale Evans was a movie and television actress, the wife of Roy Rogers, and a strong Christian woman. Dale offered a superb view on seasonal giving when she said, "Christmas, my child, is love in action. … Every time we love, every time we give, it's Christmas.

Expand your "season of giving" – make Christmas last for twelve months!

My most significant takeaways:

How I will apply this:

Other related scriptures:

21

Anger Management

Their Momma's favorite movie had been The Wizard of Oz, so it seemed only natural for her adult children to ask for the song "Over the Rainbow" to be played as their dear mother's coffin was brought into the chapel. Her children brought the soundtrack to the Nashville-area funeral home and left it with the director as details of the final arrangements were made for the next day.

At precisely 10:00 a.m., the pastor walked into the chapel, leading the two funeral assistants who were slowly rolling the casket. The funeral home director hit the "Play" button on the CD player but failed to notice he had cued up the wrong song. Instead of listening to Judy Garland wistfully singing "Over the Rainbow," the grieving family and friends were shocked to hear the Munchkins squeaking out, "Ding dong! The witch is dead. Which old witch? The wicked witch! Ding dong! The wicked witch is dead!" The family's stunned silence soon turned to white-hot anger, and within days they filed a bitter lawsuit.

In Matthew 5, Jesus spoke very directly about the topic of anger. He went immediately from talking about murderers facing judgment (v. 21) to "everyone who is angry with his brother is subject to judgment." (v. 22) The Lord's followers never saw that coming! Anger and murder lumped together for judgment? How could that be possible? What they didn't understand is that murder and anger are both issues of the heart and spirit.

Murder is an outward act that has an inward origin, springing up from an uncontrolled spirit. Anger itself is the real sin, serving as the fuse that lights the cannon. If people regularly see you like one of the cartoon characters with steam coming out of your ears, recalling David's words from Psalm 37:8 can change your behavior and then their perception of you: Refrain from anger and give up your rage; do not be agitated—it can only bring harm.

You have a new life in Jesus, so demonstrate and live that out daily. Maybe it is time to have a private funeral service. Ask God to help you bury your anger alongside your rage. Ding dong! Your life is dead! Which life? Your sinful life. Ding dong! Your sinful life is dead!

My most significant takeaways:

How I will apply this:

Other related scriptures:

22

Be Like Mike

Don Gullett was a three-sport star for the McKell High School Bull-dogs in South Shore, Kentucky. In our part of the world, his feats were legendary. He once scored 72 points in a football game as he ran for eleven touchdowns and kicked six extra points. Don's baseball prowess also shone during his high school days and ultimately led to him winning four World Series rings as a pitcher with the Cincinnati Reds and the New York Yankees in the 1970's.

During his senior year in high school, no-hitters were a regular occurrence for this overpowering athlete, so the Prichard High School Yellow Jackets were both intimidated and excited when Gullet came to Grayson, KY. With pro scouts charting every pitch, Don lived up to his advance billing as he threw yet another no-hitter. What was so funny was that after the game, Mike Burton was bragging about hitting against Gullett – he had lined a hard foul ball down the first base line!

Some years ago, a series of commercials encouraged viewers to "Be Like Mike." While they were speaking of Michael Jordan and his achievements as a basketball player, we should "Be Like Mike" Burton as we look for small successes in the midst of failure. The apostle Paul spoke about having been given a thorn in the flesh to keep him from getting conceited (a weakness). Three times he asked God to remove the thorn, but God's response was totally unexpected: "But he said to me, "My grace is sufficient for you, for my power is made perfect in weakness." (2 Cor. 12:9)

Our Father isn't looking for Christians to overwhelm the opposition like Don Gullett overwhelmed batters. God's glory shines, not through puffed-up and self-reliant superstars, but through our weak swings at life's fastballs. Only when we humbly admit our limited contribution can God use us to accomplish the most for His honor. Because of that, Paul went on to say in verse ten, "For when I am weak, then I am strong." Great things begin to happen when we are working in Christ's power and not ours.

Many batters who struck out previously get a game-winning hit the next time up. Regardless of the current outcome, find a reason to celebrate. Be like Mike!

My most significant takeaways:

How I will apply this:

Other related scriptures:

23

Beware of Dangerous People

In the 1980's, the police force of a mid-major southern city had a female police officer who obviously had been hired into the wrong job. Several partners had experienced problems working with her due to her ineptitude, and each had managed to get her passed off to another officer.

She and Jeff, her latest partner, responded to a burglary report on the west side of town. They surprised the robber, who immediately took off running. Jeff began firing his weapon at the culprit (as was allowed by law at that time) as he vainly chased the thief, who quickly outdistanced the less-than-athletic officer.

As Jeff paused to catch his breath and reload his revolver, he looked back at his partner and, to his horror, watched as she pulled an empty shell casing from her revolver. He screamed, "What are you doing?" "I'm reloadin'," she slowly responded. "Reloading? I was in front of you!!" he yelled. And she again slowly and naively replied, "I was shootin' over your shoulder, Jeff."

He left his partner right there and never worked with her again.

Admit it. Some people are just plain dangerous, including a few who can be a threat to the ministry God has called you to. Sadly, those people often fall into a group you know as "family." An executive with an international mission agency recently shared with me that many parents refuse to attend the commissioning ceremony for their own children, those newly-minted missionaries who are about to leave for their first international assignment. Why stubbornly decline? Because the parents believe their will and wants are more important than God's calling on their adult child's life.

Jesus expected this and addressed the issue in Matthew 10:37 (HCSB), saying, "The person who loves father or mother more than Me is not worthy of Me; the person who loves son or daughter more than Me is not worthy of Me."

Let me shoot straight with you: nothing should come between you and God, including family members. Guard your calling and your ministry by prioritizing your life. God first. Family second. And that faithfulness will make you worthy of Him.

My most significant takeaways:

How I will apply this:

Other related scriptures:

24

Changing the Way We Speak

The lady pleasantly greeted people as she boarded the shuttle bus, speaking with a beautiful Jamaican accent. In stark contrast, her husband's drawl told everyone he was definitely a Southerner. After chatting with them for a few minutes, I asked what prompted her to leave her native country of Jamaica. With a totally unexpected reply she said, "I am from Arkansas, not Jamaica, and I speak like this because I have a condition that is called Foreign Accent Syndrome."

She and her husband patiently explained how she began speaking incoherently one night and, thinking she had experienced a stroke, her family rushed her to the hospital. The doctors were attempting to converse with the patient when a nurse walked in, listened momentarily, and exclaimed, "She is speaking in Creole!" The nurse assumed the unplanned role of translator for the stricken woman to help her and the medical team through the testing process. A subsequent episode some time later changed her accent to Jamaican, and her accent has stabilized there.

Foreign Accent Syndrome is an extremely rare medical condition that usually results from a stroke, migraine, or head trauma. According to Wikipedia, only 62 cases have been reported between 1941 and 2009. It literally changes the way someone talks.

Someone's way of talking is also changed when they truly accept Jesus as their Savior. The desire to honor God and to be worthy of carrying the name of Christ leads us to carefully scrutinize our actions, evaluate our relationships, and even to change how we talk. Ephesians 4:29 (ESV) guides us by saying, "Let no corrupting talk come out of your mouths, but only such as is good for building up, as fits the occasion, that it may give grace to those who hear."

Your new way of speaking – with restraint, encouragement, and love – might sound like a foreign accent, even to you. Ask God to help you continue by praying Psalm 141:3 – "Set a guard, O Lord, over my mouth; keep watch over the door of my lips." And if new associates or perhaps some of your old acquaintances are not able to understand you, don't worry. Just keep speaking God's truths. The Holy Spirit will be on the scene to serve as the translator.

My most significant takeaways:

How I will apply this:

Other related scriptures:

25

Getting To Victory Lane

Lynn pulled on her red fire suit, grabbed a black helmet, and slid through the window of the iconic number 48 Lowe's Chevrolet race car. This wasn't a mere photo op – this was her opportunity to harness several hundred horsepower and go tearing around the Nashville Superspeedway at 130 miles per hour. As a woman with a burning need for speed, my wife had dreamed of this kind of adventure, and it finally came true. Back on pit row after blasting a few laps around the 1.3 miles of concrete, she climbed from the car and shook her hair out, wearing sunglasses and looking very much the part of a top-tier NASCAR driver. One of her first comments was very revealing about her experience behind the wheel: "The opening in the helmet is so small, you can see just what is right in front of you. But you have the spotter on the radio telling you where to go."

Doesn't that sound exactly like life as you walk with God? It is easy to become smugly overconfident in our knowledge and experience. Despite our limited vision, we pick a line on the track that looks good to us and take off at breakneck speed. Forget the Holy Spirit that is talking in our ear and telling us where the dangers are, where we need to move to right now, whether to speed up or slow down. After all, who needs a spotter when you have this much skill and maturity to offer? During the excitement of the moment, we forget the directives given during the drivers' meeting before hitting the track: "Listen to your spotter and follow their instructions." God actually talked about this in Ezekiel 12:2 (NCV), saying, "Human, you are living among a people who refuse to obey. They have eyes to see, but they do not see, and they have ears to hear, but they do not hear, because they are a people who refuse to obey."

Drivers who ignore the spotter's commands get black-flagged and sent back to the pits where a stern discussion is coming from the race director. Likewise, getting to Victory Lane in life ultimately comes down to trusting the One who sees everything. Father, help us not rely upon our restricted perspective. Teach us instead to listen to our Counselor, trusting wholeheartedly in His guidance.

2 Corinthians 5:7 (HCSB) is crystal clear: "For we walk by faith, not by sight."

My most significant takeaways:

How I will apply this:

Other related scriptures:

26

Gloom, Despair, and
Agony on Me

Debbie Watts had the delightful opportunity to work with the cast of the "Hee Haw" television program for several years, seeing and interacting with the stars and celebrities on a personal level. One day at the studio, "Goober" George Lindsey snuck up behind Debbie and playfully bumped her knee from behind, causing her to slightly lurch forward. Without even glancing behind her, she reactively swung with a mighty backhand that was right on target. The crafty "Goober" ducked, though, and with perfect show-biz timing, Debbie got the attention of Grandpa Jones when she caught him with full force "up the side of his head," as we say here in the South. Imagine his surprise – and Debbie's – when his head went flying one way and his fake mustache went flying another! Fortunately, Grandpa Jones forgave her, and they became great friends.

God sometimes smacks us "up the side of our head" to get our attention, to awaken us from the numbing routines that lead us to put family, work, and ministry on autopilot. As Grandpa Jones would have agreed, that can be painful. Scripture tells us, "Hard times and trouble are God's way of getting our attention!" (Job 36:15 CEV) A recurring Hee Haw segment featured four male cast members who told of their woeful life by mournfully singing, "Gloom, despair, agony on me; Deep dark depression, excessive misery." Sound like your theme song? Just understand you aren't performing a solo since at some point, probably every one of us chimes in with a verse of two of that sad tune.

When trouble smacks you hard, your choice is clear: either ask God what He wants you to learn from this event, or get angry and blame God, yourself, and anyone else that comes to mind. The second response is our knee-jerk, instinctive reaction, but the first is of much greater benefit. Job 36:16 explains why: "And at this very moment, God deeply desires to lead you from trouble and to spread your table with your favorite food" (CEV).

When God gets your attention, put your false pride (and false mustache) aside and look for the lesson. Be reachable, teachable, and "know that God is always at work for the good of everyone who loves him" (Romans 8:28 CEV).

My most significant takeaways:

How I will apply this:

Other related scriptures:

27

Holding On To Hope

Four-letter words are often viewed with a negative slant. That dubious reputation is probably deservedly assigned. Other four-letter words bring a burst of positivity with them. Such is the case with the word "hope". A great emphasis is placed on the desperate need for children to have hope. Hope for a dreamed-of career. Hope for an adoptive home to open up. Hope for just one meal to quiet the hunger that is always present.

Even for adults, hopes can soar. Unless they are dashed. Debbie Yokely of the Alabama Adult Education shared a story about an adult education counselor who once told a student he would never amount to anything. Fast forward several years, and while on a skiing trip to Colorado, the counselor took a tumble down the slope and broke her leg. She and her family decided to return to sweet home Alabama for her surgery.

At the hospital on the morning of the operation, the nurses got her settled into the pre-op room. A gentleman in scrubs walked in and intently studied her chart. He looked at her and said, "You don't remember me, do you? You told me I would never amount to anything, and guess what? I'm your anesthesiologist, and now I'm about to put you under!"

Christians have soaring hopes as well, but sometimes our expectations are slammed into the rocky shoreline. As we watch the onslaught of attacks against our faith, as we hear reports of our brothers and sisters in Christ being martyred for their faith, our hopes for the world can become dimmed. Losing faith, though, is not in the DNA of our calling. 2 Corinthians 4:16 (ESV) renews our confidence and optimism: "So we do not lose heart. Though our outer self is wasting away, our inner self is being renewed day by day."

God never promised a smooth, uninterrupted ride through life – via bus, ski slopes, or any other means. Those faithful to the Lord can count on the outcome, though, and it isn't a hope – it is a promise. In the interim, simply follow the instructions contained in Romans 12:12 (ESV) – "Rejoice in hope, be patient in tribulation, be constant in prayer."

My most significant takeaways:

How I will apply this:

Other related scriptures:

28

Major Mistakes

Making mistakes is something everyone has done, but some of them are real doozies that make us feel extremely foolish. Lauren went with some friends to a local nightspot for a girl's night out of fun and free-flowing adult beverages. At one point during the evening, Lauren went to the ladies room to freshen up, and she discovered several cosmetic and styling products available for the club's female guests. Lauren re-styled her hair, picked up a can, and carefully misted the new look. Immediately her locks fell away from the styling she had just done! Once more she styled, sprayed, and watched her hair fall. She repeated the process a third time, with the same lackluster result. As she furiously applied a heavier coating of spray on the fourth attempt, a lady who had been watching the entire time casually commented, "Honey, I think you have enough deodorant on your hair now."

Mistakes in the things we do are troubling and embarrassing enough, but some of our greatest mistakes are the things we say. The Bible talks about that in James 3:2 (NLT) in saying, "Indeed, we all make many mistakes. For if we could control our tongues, we would be perfect and could also control ourselves in every other way." Oh, if people could only control their tongues! There is a vast array of things we could say, just sitting there in front of us, and often we thoughtlessly grab one and go to work.

It is easy to snatch up a can of Anger – or of Calm. Read the label to see if you picked up a bottle of Belittling or of Building Up. We can apply a few squirts of Hatred or a dash of Helpfulness. Tempted to splash on some Stinging Sarcasm before meeting with that loser co-worker? Opt for the wonderful fragrance of Respect instead. Spit out your Bitter Outrage mouthwash and change instead to one flavored with Patience. A little diligence helps us avoid our verbal mistakes.

A father was helping his son work on a truck late one night. Dad started the truck, and they labored quite a while longer as they tested and adjusted before finally quitting for the night. When Dad walked outside the next morning, the truck engine was running – as it had been all night! Yes, we all make mistakes. Let's just test and adjust our tongues to keep them from running when they shouldn't.

My most significant takeaways:

How I will apply this:

Other related scriptures:

29

The Joy of Peace
and Quiet

Finding a few moments of simple peace and quiet can be an elusive goal. Today's world seems intent on providing a never-ending flow of chatter and noise that feels impossible to escape. The auditory onslaught can become absolutely maddening.

While vacationing a few years ago in Pagosa Springs, Colorado, I saw a flyer for a company that offered hot air balloon rides. The idea of serenely floating above the breathtaking Rocky Mountain countryside was irresistible, so I scheduled an early-morning ride. My anticipation of drifting high above the ground in tranquility soon came crashing earthward. The balloon pilot talked almost non-stop for the hour-long flight, providing an ongoing narrative of historical commentary and geographical information. I wanted to scream, "Would you please just shut up!!?"

Others want quiet as well. Ron Holloway's great-grandfather, Jim, lived in a little shotgun house in East Nashville around 1916. The couple next door fought bitterly and frequently, and one day their son came flying through Jim's front door, breathlessly saying, "Mr. Marshall, you've got to come. You've got to come quick." Jim followed the boy and ran to the next house, where he discovered a gruesome scene. His neighbor's wife was lying on the kitchen floor in a pool of blood with a hatchet sticking out of her head. Her husband looked up and quietly repeated over and over, "Jim, she wouldn't shut up; she just wouldn't shut up."

Today, peace and quiet and wishing the world would just shut up, even briefly, might be at the very top of the Christmas wish list for many. Mental restoration and refreshment occurs during times of stillness. More importantly, those moments allow us the opportunity to talk with our Creator. In Psalm 46:10 (ESV), God directs, "Be still, and know that I am God. I will be exalted among the nations, I will be exalted in the earth!" Silence is golden. Even brief escapes from the acoustic avalanche provide us the wonderful opportunity to "Be still, and know that He is God," letting us strive to hear His voice and know His heart.

The heavenly choir sang to celebrate the birth of Jesus, the Prince of Peace. And then everyone basked in the peacefulness of the glorious night. "Silent night, holy night; all is calm, all is bright."

May your life be filled with peace and quiet.

My most significant takeaways:

How I will apply this:

Other related scriptures:

30

How to Break Your Fall

Brian Brown and I headed out for an early-morning adventure at an indoor paintball range. Friendly paintball competition is great fun and typically very safe. That day was different. Paintballs are made with a vegetable oil base, and the splatters that hit the concrete floor of this converted manufacturing plant created a super-slippery surface. Instead of quickly darting from one room or protective barrier to another, we found ourselves slowly creeping along much like actor Tim Conway in his role as the tottering old man. Flash back to your worst experience ever attempting to walk across ice, and you will understand our precarious dilemma. At one point, Brian's feet suddenly went one direction without giving advance notice to the rest of his body, and he crashed hard. He later mentioned that his side was hurting, but it took a trip to the hospital to confirm a broken rib.

The falls we experience aren't always physical in nature. People fall ill, fall in with the wrong crowd, or fall into disgrace. We are told if we fall in line, things in life will fall in place. We fall all over ourselves when we fall under someone's captivating spell and fall in love. And sometimes we fall on hard times.

During WWII, military aviator Louis Zamperini's plane fell from the sky and crashed into the Pacific Ocean. He promised to give his life to God if the Lord would just free him from this ordeal. Psalm 34:17

offers hope during our trials when it says, "The righteous cry out, and the Lord hears, and delivers them from all their troubles." What a comforting thought! The Lord heard Louis, like He hears us. After forty-seven incredibly harsh days in a life raft, Zamperini was indeed rescued – by the enemy Japanese, who imprisoned and brutally tortured him in a prisoner-of-war camp. That outcome probably wasn't what Zamperini envisioned as he prayed and asked for deliverance from his troubles.

Death, pain, and suffering are the result from the fall of mankind in the Garden of Eden, but God offers daily hope in James 1:12 (HCSB) when He says: "A man who endures trials is blessed, because when he passes the test he will receive the crown of life that God has promised to those who love Him."

Passing the test is as easy as falling off a log: repent and call on the name of Jesus. When we do, God will never fall short on fulfilling His pledge of deliverance for us.

My most significant takeaways:

How I will apply this:

Other related scriptures:

31

Just When I Need Him Most

Simply bending over to get an item from my briefcase on the floor had thrown my back out that morning. Unable to straighten up fully, I labored through the pain and the hours to finish the seminar I was conducting in Miami. Wrestling a fully-loaded suitcase out of the rental car and into the airport terminal only added to my misery at the end of the day. I got through security, boarded the aircraft, and then slowly and agonizingly crammed myself into the tiny seat. The pain intensified, and no amount of movement or adjusting offered any relief. Two and one-half hours of throbbing discomfort lay between me and getting home to Nashville.

Then the flight attendant showed up, smiling brightly as she said, "Mr. Richmond, we have the upgrade to first class that you requested." My shocked response was to ask my seatmate his name. Why? It had to be his upgrade since I had not requested an upgrade. She couldn't have possibly meant me. Or could she? Thankfully, his name was not Richmond, and I was on my way to a real seat and real relaxation. The flight home was wonderful, with absolutely no back discomfort until I stood again when we landed.

God knows exactly what we need and when we need it most. When Adam needed a mate, God made Eve. When the Hebrews faced a wall of water as they escaped from Egypt, Jehovah provided a walk-through aquarium. When Daniel needed a rescuer, Jehovah sent an angel (and maybe duct tape?) to close the lion's mouth. The significance of the Lord's provision is so important it is captured in the only miracle recorded in all four Gospels: when Jesus fed the 5,000 followers (probably 20,000 including women and children). Whatever your needs are, God already knows. Philippians 4:19 (AMP) explains the fulfillment when Paul says, "And my God will liberally supply (fill until full) your every need according to His riches in glory in Christ Jesus."

God knew my need and provided for my need, for immediate relief from the pain. I had not asked Him or the airline for first class, and still He filled me with comfort for the duration of the flight. When you truly need Him most, just remember the beautiful words written by David in Psalm 23: "The Lord is my Shepherd, I shall not want."

My most significant takeaways:

How I will apply this:

Other related scriptures:

32

Pastor Appreciation

Dr. Thom Rainer, President of LifeWay Christian Resources, recently conducted a Twitter poll of unusual things people say to pastors. The responses ranged from humorous to downright wacky. (Makes you wonder about the people sitting in the pews...) Anyway, enjoy the comments and Dr. Rainer's reflections on them.

- "Do you grow weed in your closet?" (The church member actually wanted to look in the pastor's closet to confirm his suspicions.)
- "Sorry I was late to church. My dog, Rambo, and I have been witnessing to people." (Rambo must be a special dog.)
- "I don't know if I will be able to help with baptism tomorrow. I'm bleeding from my rectum. I think it's hemorrhoids." (By all means, please stay home.)
- "Are you the one who keeps taking the beer off my daddy's grave?" (I'm left wondering how daddy gets the beer.)
- "So did you fly or drive there?" (That was a question asked of a pastor after he returned from a trip to the continent of Africa.)
- "We never had these storms until you came." (Those are words said to a pastor after hurricanes Rita and Ike.)
- "You blink too much when you preach. You are also a very pale person." (Thank you for your kind words.)

- "Top that, preacher!" (Words spoken to the pastor by the soloist as she stepped down from the podium.)
- "I need you to go catch a peacock that escaped!" (Of course, that's item 6c in the job description.)
- "I can tell you have the anointing of God. My cat does too." (It must be a very spirited cat.)
- "You need to wear a bra when you preach." (Just to be clear, this statement was said to a male preacher.)

October is Pastor Appreciation Month. Please take the time to let the shepherd of your flock know just how much you appreciate him. After all, they are following the Lord's call on their life, as expressed in 1 Peter 5:2: "Be shepherds of God's flock that is under your care, watching over them – not because you must, but because you are willing, as God wants you to be."

My most significant takeaways:

How I will apply this:

Other related scriptures:

33

Showers of Blessings

There was nothing extraordinary about this particular chapel service at the assisted living facility, no indication in advance of the special gifts that were about to be exchanged. Just a typical day and a typical service. To begin my message, I asked an open-ended question to some of the residents who were sitting near the front. Jane Davis was one of those who responded, and we spent a few moments in dialogue concerning her response and how that aligned with the scripture text. I continued with my sermon, and we closed with a final song and a prayer.

After the chapel time was wrapped up, a lady named Barbara Sullivan sought me out. She had been sitting with Jane, and Barbara said, "I just want you to know that my mother has dementia. She hasn't spoken like that to anyone in two years. Thank you so much."

It is a good thing that I am not a weather man because my forecast of "Just a typical day and a typical service" was woefully inaccurate. When we obediently serve the Lord, chances are we will never know nor fully understand the depths of the blessings others receive. I was deeply moved and humbled to know God had used me in those brief moments to spread a beam of sunlight into Barbara's life.

Proverbs 11:24 (ESV) explains the concept in saying, "One gives freely, yet grows all the richer." At that moment, it felt as good as if an armored truck had pulled up and unloaded a million dollars at my feet.

Serving is not intended to be an action motivated by the rewards we might receive. Hebrews 13:16 (ESV) tells us, "Do not neglect to do good and to share what you have, for such sacrifices are pleasing to God."

Far too many of our days are invested in studying the horizons of our lives, watching for storm clouds that at times blot out the sun and threaten to engulf us. We, as Christ's followers, should instead decide to be involved with showers of blessings. Choose "to do good and to share what you have," and God will use your service to demonstrate His love and to bless others.

When you follow God's plan, I predict a one-hundred percent chance of showers of blessings falling on your life as well.

My most significant takeaways:

How I will apply this:

Other related scriptures:

34

Critical Words

We might not recognize it at that precise moment we speak, but critical words do not follow Dale Carnegie's recipe on how to win friends and influence people.

Leon Kilbreth was known as Mr. Sunday School for his extraordinary work in developing programs in many churches. He also served for many years as a football official. During one game, Leon threw a penalty flag on one team, sending the coach into a tirade. His outburst toward Leon concluded with the parting shot, "Ref, you stink!" Mr. Sunday School quickly threw another penalty flag and moved farther from the coach as he stepped off the fifteen-yard penalty. He then called back toward the coach, "Do I smell any better from here?"

In another instance, Dale Lingenfelter was the coach who lost his cool. In all his years coaching basketball, he said only one technical foul was called on him for unsportsmanlike conduct. His overreach? Dale heatedly barked at the referee, "That thing in your mouth is a whistle, not an all-day sucker! You ought to blow it sometimes, not just suck on it!!!" (The ref blew the whistle when he teed Dale up.)

One website warns believers to beware of a having a critical spirit: "There is a significant difference between helping someone improve and having a critical spirit. A critical spirit is never pleased. A critical spirit expects and finds disappointment wherever it looks. It is the opposite of 1 Corinthians 13: a critical spirit arrogantly judges, is easily provoked, accounts for every wrong, and never carries any hope of being pleased. Such an attitude damages the critiqued as well as the critic."

Would you best be described as helpful or harping? Cheerful or critical? A lady once complained about her spouse, "Some days Hitler would be Santa Claus compared to my husband!" Ouch! Don't be that person. Instead, daily consider how you can live out the instructions of 2 Timothy 2:24-25 "The Lord's slave must not quarrel, but must be gentle to everyone, able to teach, and patient, instructing his opponents with gentleness." (HCSB)

Ask the Lord to help you build up instead of tear down. Your encouraging and supportive approach goes a long way toward winning friends and influencing people for Christ.

My most significant takeaways:

How I will apply this:

Other related scriptures:

35

Return on Investment

And he said to them, "Go into all the world and proclaim the gospel to the whole creation. (Mark 16:15 ESV)

Proclaiming the gospel. Some find the prospect frightening. Others find it exhilarating. For Charles Hand, talking about Jesus was as natural as breathing. Cancer gave him just another reason to talk. Not about death. About eternal life.

The physicians at the Veterans Administration hospital in Oklahoma City rotate regularly. They typically spend about two weeks before moving on to other patients, and Charles' oncologist was nearing the end of his tour of duty with this particular group. As he walked into the hospital room, Charles greeted him quickly and then immediately began sharing the gospel with him. The physician listened briefly before replying, "Oh yeah. I was saved as a six-year-old boy." Charles inquired, "Really? Tell me about that."

His doctor said, "Well, I lived in Indiana." Charles interrupted, "Wow. I used to live in Indiana." The doctor continued, "Somebody came by my home on Saturday and asked my mother if I could ride the bus to Sunday School. My mother agreed, so the next morning I got up and rode that bus to Sunday School. My Sunday School teacher brought a lesson that morning on how to be saved. At the close of the class, I told my teacher I wanted to do that. I prayed to receive Christ. I was just that little six-year-old boy."

He continued, "My Sunday School teacher came out to my house the next week, talked to my mother about what I had done, and talked to my mother about me being baptized. I was baptized at that church just two or three weeks after that."

Charles asked him, "Where was that?" The doc answered, "Well, it was called Hammond, and it was in First Baptist Church in Hammond, Indiana." Still probing, Charles queried, "What year was that?" The physician thoughtfully studied for a moment and said, "Well, let me see. Here is how old I am, and I was six years old. That was 1965."

Charles paused for a moment, took a deep breath, and answered, "Well, you would probably be really interested in knowing that in 1965, I started that bus ministry at First Baptist Church in Hammond."

Mike Hand is Charles' son, and today he serves as a Partnership Missions Strategist with the Baptist General Convention of Oklahoma. As he proudly shared this very personal story, he observed, "What are the chances of a guy meeting a guy and his salvation going back to a church where this guy was on staff fifty-one years ago? What are the odds or the chances of a guy that was saved because of a ministry this other guy started fifty-one years ago, and they both don't even live in the same community any longer?"

A new life was born. Charles Hand's investment of time yielded a return that will last forever. God's perfect will was demonstrated yet again.

"In the same way, let your light shine before others, so that they may see your good works and give glory to your Father who is in heaven." (Matthew 5:16)

My most significant takeaways:

How I will apply this:

Other related scriptures:

36

Sound Off

Our son, Brett, vacationed in Panama City, Florida a few years ago. One day a man approached him and asked, "Are you Chief Richmond's son?" Brett was over 450 miles from home, and still he was instantly identified by someone I had served with at nearby Tyndall Air Force Base. When my daughter posted a photo of her grandfather on Facebook, many thought the picture was of me. The family line is evident.

Whom do you look like? Perhaps more importantly, whom do you sound like? Lynn and I met a man in Baltimore who sounds exactly like actor Morgan Freeman. This week I met retired Metro Nashville police officer Bill Dillon, who sounds just like the character Tobias Fornell on the "NCIS" television show.

When you speak, whom do you sound like? Crabby neighbor or caring co-worker? A hothead or a helpful friend? Are you mean-spirited or well-meaning? Do you come across as unhinged or unruffled? Those burning questions set the stage for the biggie: Do you sound like a jerk or like Jesus? After all, the apostle John said, "Whoever says he abides in him ought to walk in the same way in which he walked." (1 John 2:6 ESV) As Christians, this should be our daily goal.

Life can be tough. Situations exceed challenging. We might try to blame those circumstances for our short-fuse. A lady named Gayle Urban was shopping in a Christian bookstore and discovered a shelf of reduced-price items. Among the gifts was a little figurine of a man and woman, their heads lovingly tilted toward one another. HAPPY 10th ANNIVERSARY read the inscription. It appeared to be in perfect condition, yet its tag indicated "Damaged." Examining it more closely, she found another tag underneath that read "Wife is Coming Unglued."

Whether in a marriage, a friendship, or a workplace, words serve like bricks to build a relationship. Or like bombs to destroy it. Want to influence people for Christ? James, brother of Jesus, and the apostle Paul gave comparable instructions: "If anyone thinks he is religious and does not bridle his tongue but deceives his heart, this person's religion is worthless. You must put them all away: anger, wrath, malice, slander, and obscene talk from your mouth." (James 1:26; Colossians 3:8)

Ultimately it doesn't matter if you sound like Merle Haggard or Dolly Parton or Richard Nixon. The only question that matters is, "Do I sound like Jesus?"

My most significant takeaways:

How I will apply this:

Other related scriptures:

37

Thanksgiving Is a Good Obsession

Don Vicars, an Oregon police officer, was on his way to California for a Harley Davidson convention when a construction zone caused a group of motorcycles to stop suddenly. Don had to lay his motorcycle down at high speed and was left with a broken shoulder, broken ribs, and a collapsed lung.

A passerby stopped to aid Vicars. She told him her name was Sally, adding that she was a registered nurse. She cradled him in his pain and assured him that help was on the way. When paramedics arrived, Vicars was airlifted to a hospital where he spent ten days. After her compassionate act, Don was intent on finding and thanking Sally.

"When I woke up on the pavement," he said, "she was holding my head. She very calmly talked to me and calmed me. Afterward, she just walked off. It's important to me to find her and thank her."

Vicars' wife said her husband's need to find Sally was "almost an obsession." In a newspaper article in The Oregonian (10/15/98), Vicars asked that anyone who knew Sally would contact him.

Thanksgiving is a good obsession.

People can become obsessed with virtually anything. Worry, work, or the weather. Family, fun, or the future. Collections, contamination, or loss of control. Of all people, Christians have a reason to be obsessed – with thanksgiving. David said it perfectly in Psalm 28:7 (ESV): "The Lord is my strength and my shield; in him my heart trusts, and I am helped; my heart exults, and with my song I give thanks to him." My strength and my shield. Oh yes, I'm thankful!

As you gather with family and friends to celebrate Thanksgiving Day, remember to offer thanks for even the small things in life. One lady shared a wonderful example, saying, "As our family was enjoying a delicious Thanksgiving dinner, my four-year-old granddaughter stopped chomping on her drumstick long enough to look at her mother, smile, and say, 'I really like turkey on the cob.'"

Become obsessed. "Give thanks in everything." (1 Thessalonians 5:18 HCSB)

My most significant takeaways:

How I will apply this:

Other related scriptures:

38

I've Got a Secret

Country music superstar Martina McBride was featured on the SiriusXM Town Hall show as they celebrated her twenty-five years in the industry. Host Storme Warren went through the routine "How would you describe the journey?" type of questions before he got to one that was off the beaten path. His query of "What is something people don't know about you?" initially stumped his guest. Martina said, "I think they know everything about me. After all, I've been at this twenty-five years." Then she blurted out, "Oh, I like the toilet paper underneath on the roll. I'm an underneath toilet paper girl."

Storme could never have anticipated hearing that answer, but he countered quickly, "Do you ever go to a friend's house and, if their toilet paper is over the top, change it?" "Absolutely!" Martina replied. "I HAVE to. It's almost a superstitious thing with me."

Is there something people don't know about you? What about the dark secrets, those hidden items you hope no one ever discovers? For example, Alfred Hitchcock, the master of gripping suspense, was reported to be afraid of eggs. People go to incredible lengths to keep certain elements of their life or their past buried. We believe and profusely hope no one knows. And that belief is incorrect.

"Lord, you have examined me and know all about me. You know when I sit down and when I get up. You know my thoughts before I think them. You know where I go and where I lie down. You know everything I do. Lord, even before I say a word, you already know it." (Psalm 139:1-4, NCV)

Years ago Cincinnati newspapers reported that a shabbily dressed woman went to Dr. George Herman and asked him to X-ray her heart for free. She claimed she was very poor and couldn't afford to pay. The generous doctor agreed to treat this destitute lady, but when he turned his X-ray machine a little below her heart, he saw a concealed pocket in her blouse which contained five twenty-dollar gold pieces. After the examination, the woman asked what Dr. Herman had discovered. "Your heart is very bad," he said. "You lied when you said you were poor."

Toilet paper direction doesn't matter. Lord, reveal the secrets I hide even from myself. Show me where I am poor in spirit when your riches are so near my heart.

My most significant takeaways:

How I will apply this:

Other related scriptures:

39

Memorable Meetings

Rick wiped the tears from his eyes. His 54-year-old wife of nine years had died just minutes before. My words of consolation as a hospice chaplain went unheard. His pain was too overwhelming. The presence of another human being offered greater comfort. I stood silently as he sorted through his emotions. Then he smiled.

"Did I tell you how I met my wife? You won't believe this. We met at a WalMart in Mississippi, not far from Memphis. My mother and I had gone to the store for something. We needed help finding whatever it was, and this lady assisted us. She was really nice. I took my mother home and told her, 'I'm going back to the store. I liked that lady.' I got there and finally found her. When I came up behind her, I didn't quite know what to say,…so I hit her in the back of the head with a bag of marshmallows!"

Memorable meetings. What do people remember you for? Maybe it is your face. In all its glory, your mug serves as a very memorable business card. God has a suggestion to aid the moment. Proverbs 15:13 (MSG) reads, "A cheerful heart brings a smile to your face." Yes, I get it that things are tough sometimes. The psalmist answers, "O my soul, why be so gloomy and discouraged? Trust in God! I shall again praise him for his wondrous help; he will make me smile again, for he is my God!" (Psalm 43:5 TLB).

Every encounter with a person can be memorable. If done the right way.

Sandy laughed as she told of what was probably her most embarrassing moment ever. She said, "You remember Jimmy Stewart, don't you? (Me – "Of course!") Well, I got to go to Jimmy Stewart's 75th birthday party! It was so exciting when Jimmy Stewart arrived with his wife. He is tall! Anyway, Mr. Stewart and his wife were standing at the top of the stairs. He looked so handsome and debonair up there, and I wanted to meet him.

"I ran up the stairs, and I was going to shake his hand, and then at the last second I decided to hug him. Then I tripped on the last step and crashed into Jimmy Stewart and knocked him down! He got up and dusted himself off, straightened out the rumples in his jacket, and said, 'Ma'am, I love that my fans love me, but please, don't kill me on my birthday!'"

Be memorable. For your smile. For your joy. For being a bright light. For bringing hope. Why go to that much effort?

For God so loved the world.

My most significant takeaways:

How I will apply this:

Other related scriptures:

40

Dancing to Our Own Music

Ah, the days of being sixteen years old. Young, carefree, and impulsive. It was that mile-wide streak of impulsiveness that often got us into our biggest jams.

Back when she was sixteen, Betty Smith, her friend, Carol, and their dates were headed for the Belle Meade Motel Restaurant. The eatery had a little three-piece band each Friday and Saturday night, and these young adults loved going there to dance. Unfortunately, they discovered the restaurant was closed for remodeling. Now what? One of the boys said, "I know a place that has a juke box and a nice little dance floor," so off the foursome went.

Their destination was a dive called PeeWee's, a hole-in-the-wall joint off Nolensville Road near the Nashville Fairgrounds. While not an establishment any of their parents would have approved of, the headstrong foursome was not to be deterred. They waltzed in like they owned the place, plugged coins into the juke box, and had a great time dancing on the little twelve feet by sixteen feet floor.

And then the front door burst open.

Carol's father purposefully strode through the door like a man on a mission, spying them instantly. He hissed, "What are you kids doing here?" Dancing," came their whispered reply. Dad barked, "Out the back door! Now!!!" Betty and Carol grabbed their purses, and just as they went out the back door, a flood of police officers swarmed through the front door to raid PeeWee's.

Carol's dad, a Nashville police detective, had saved their bacon. All four of those teenagers might still be doing hard time in the slammer if a loving father had not rescued them. As much as that detective was concerned about Carol and her friends, God loves you even more than that.

God has come to save me. I will trust in him and not be afraid. The LORD rescues the godly; he is their fortress in times of trouble. He has rescued us from the kingdom of darkness and transferred us into the Kingdom of his dear Son. Give your burdens to the LORD, and he will take care of you. (Isaiah 12:2; Psalm 37:39; Colossians 1:13; Psalm 55:22 NLT)

Like Betty and Carol, our impulsiveness leads us to dance to our own music. Thankfully, our loving and gracious Father has rescued us from the eternal sentence that would otherwise await us. Trust in Him. He has come to save you.

My most significant takeaways:

How I will apply this:

Other related scriptures:

41

Follow the Leader

After much disappointment in applying for summer work after graduating high school, Tess Longmire finally got a job. It wasn't on her Top Ten list of desired positions. In fact, she really didn't want this position at all. Working in a day care – and especially working with kids – felt like something akin to a prison sentence.

On her first day in the corporate world, Tess honestly told the Director of her lack of experience, including having done absolutely no babysitting. "You'll be fine!" came the quick and confident reply. In no time, Tess found herself trapped, alone and very uncertain, in a room with seven menacing two-year olds.

Things went reasonably well until one free-spirited child determined he needed fewer restraints in life. "Nick" proceeded to undress himself, removing every stitch of his clothing, including his Huggies loincloth. Since Tess had not seen any signs indicating the day care was clothing-optional, she uncertainly collected the bare-bottomed buckaroo and his clothing. Beginning the arduous task of diapering a wiggly, unwilling tot, Tess glanced up – and in horror saw four of the other children had joined Nick in his protest by removing all of their clothing as well!

Just like little Nick, people are watching you. No, I am not speaking of the video surveillance cameras that now populate many homes, businesses, and roadways. There are random individuals who watch our individual actions. Whether we want to accept the responsibility or not, there is a distinct possibility they will copy what they see. You and I are starring in our own reality show, and the reality is that our actions will be imitated by some of our audience members. They decide to follow the leader. Professor Howard Hendricks of Dallas Theological Seminary once wrote there were one hundred or so leaders in the Bible, two-thirds of whom did not finish well. The apostle Paul was a tremendous leader who did finish well, and his inspired words provide a road map that can keep us and our actions on track:

Therefore, since we also have such a large cloud of witnesses surrounding us, let us lay aside every weight and the sin that so easily ensnares us. Let us run with endurance the race that lies before us, keeping our eyes on Jesus. (Hebrews 12:1-2 HCSB)

People may have 500 cable channels and still find nothing worth watching. Nick and you and I, on the other hand, are of great interest to them. Since they tune into your reality channel, "you yourself must be an example to them of good deeds of every kind" (Titus 2:7 TLB). Be a leader whose life is worthy of following.

My most significant takeaways:

How I will apply this:

Other related scriptures:

42

Giving the Right Gifts

When my son was about ten years old, we were visiting with my mother for Christmas. Brett eagerly tore into his first gift from Granny – and was visibly stunned to find a little, yellow Playskool bus that had the open top so you could put in and take out the little school children figurines. One quick (and stern) look at him quickly communicated, "Don't you dare say a word!"

We give gifts daily. Family, friends, co-workers, the neighbor across the street. All receive them. But, like Brett, are they actually thrilled to receive our gifts? Would they have much preferred something else instead?

The questions are valid. You and I hand-pick and then personally deliver those gifts, so shouldn't they be the best available? It might help if we incorporate more thoughtful planning into our gift-selecting process. After all, ten-year-old boys do not want preschool toys. With that in mind, picture yourself walking down a store's aisle. Gifts of one category on the left; the second category on the right.

Love...or lack of concern.
Caring...or a crusty demeanor.
Sharing...or snubbing.
Helping...or hurrying away.

Praying...or just promising to.

Gratitude...or grumpiness.

Smile...or a scowl.

Kindness...or indifference.

Friendship...or frostiness.

Listening...or looking at your watch.

The right gifts...or the wrong gifts.

Do not neglect to do good and to share what you have, for such sacrifices are pleasing to God. Each one must give as he has decided in his heart...for God loves a cheerful giver. Remember the words of the Lord Jesus... 'It is more blessed to give than to receive.' (Heb. 13:16; 2 Cor. 9:7; Acts 20:35 ESV)

Our best and most carefully selected gifts, though, never approach the magnitude of the greatest gift ever: "For God so loved the world in this way: He gave His One and Only Son." (John 3:16 HCSB)

Choose gifts that reflect the Son who was given for us.

My most significant takeaways:

How I will apply this:

Other related scriptures:

43

In Other Words

Words are one of our most valuable commodities. They express love, form requests, and voice joy or pain. Words convey vision and hope, limits and despair. Words are sometimes used for good-natured teasing. Words say a lot to someone, and they also express a lot about the speaker.

Drew, a good old boy lineman for AT&T, has an ample physique that would best be described as an upside-down muffin. Appearing more flab than fit, he smiled as he told that his wife describes him as "muscle bound." Drew patted his oversized stomach and paused for effect, laughing as he continued, "She says there's bound to be a muscle in there somewhere!"

Some words are fun. Others are no laughing matter. Bruce Damrow is a long-time friend who, after retiring, became a member of a local zoning board. A nearby church had opened an alcohol and drug rehab center on their fifty-plus acres about six months earlier, but it had neglected to apply for the proper zoning variance. A public hearing was held to allow local residents to offer their position concerning the new facility. At least six people approached the microphone and began their comments with the words, "I am a Christian, but..." Each then went on to bluntly state their opposition to a rehab center. Bruce quizzed the group, "Since the center opened six months ago, have there been any problems? Have they caused any trouble? Have the police been called for any reason?" Their subdued response to each question was "No." Still, their opposition never wavered. Their faith fell victim to their fears. An important question to consider is, what would Jesus say?

For I was hungry and you gave me something to eat, I was thirsty and you gave me something to drink, I was a stranger and you invited me in, I needed clothes and you clothed me, I was sick and you looked after me, I was in prison and you came to visit me.'

"Then the righteous will answer him, 'Lord, when did we see you hungry and feed you, or thirsty and give you something to drink? When did we see you a stranger and invite you in, or needing clothes and clothe you? When did we see you sick or in prison and go to visit you?'

"The King will reply, 'Truly I tell you, whatever you did for one of the least of these brothers and sisters of mine, you did for me.' (Matthew 25:35-40 NIV)

"I am a Christian, but..." One revealing phrase. Five dangerous words. Let's decide to replace that phrase with seven words that reflect the Lord's heart: "Jesus loves you. How can I help?"

My most significant takeaways:

How I will apply this:

Other related scriptures:

44

It Seemed Like a Good Idea at the Time

For all of our grand ideas, everyone has at least one idea that is a royal dud. Rev. Ron Hardeman had his own spectacular, bad-idea moment a number of years ago at a church he was leading. He decided to forego the usual Sunday evening worship service and instead have a member-led singing time.

Anyone who wanted was allowed to come to the microphone and sing. Not many were willing, but one bold six-year-old boy seized the opportunity. Rev. Ron said he couldn't quite understand what the boy was singing as the lad somewhat mumbled through the first verse. The aspiring vocalist's delivery soared, however, when he got to the chorus as he confidently and loudly belted out, "You gotta know when to hold 'em, know when to fold 'em, know when to walk away, know when to run..." (Bro. Ron said that it was perhaps the most spiritual song he had ever heard in church.)

If there is any area of our lives where absolute caution is requisite, it is our faith. New ideas and approaches require careful consideration to see how they measure up against Biblical teaching. Scripture guides us, "My people are destroyed for lack of knowledge. See to it that no one takes you captive by philosophy and empty deceit. Beloved, do not believe every spirit, but test the spirits to see whether they are from God, for many false prophets have gone out into the world. Ignorant people and people who aren't sure of what they believe distort what Paul says in his letters the same way they distort the rest of the Scriptures. (Hosea 4:6; Colossians 2:8; 1 John 4:1 ESV; 2 Peter 3:16 GW).

History demonstrates that some ideas like telephones and personal computers have proven to be truly outstanding, while other ideas leave us scratching our head in wonderment. For example, 20th Century Fox signed over all merchandising rights for any and all Star Wars films to George Lucas for a mere $20,000 cut in Lucas' studio paycheck. Lucas' return on that investment? It is estimated over three billion dollars' worth of merchandise has been sold.

The latest bad idea I heard about? At Baker's Bay Golf and Ocean Club in Abaco, Bahamas, golfers are allowed to play shirtless. The reported pros of this concept include beating the summer heat, as well as providing a more relaxed environment. Some of the cons include players discovering the oddity of seeing their stomachs as they address the ball. What is even worse is that with plenty of spots to grab a cocktail on the course, the more people drink, the more clothes come off. Ewww! Know when to walk away. Know when to run.

"See to it that no one takes you captive by philosophy and empty deceit."

My most significant takeaways:

How I will apply this:

Other related scriptures:

45

Little Things Make a Huge Difference

Rev. Andrew Jensen's first Sunday at his new church came on the same day as an appeal from the church to the membership to donate to a fund to aid the victims of a hurricane. Due to a clerical error, the center page of the bulletin was missing, so those in attendance reading from the bottom of the second page to the top of the last page would have read:

"Welcome to the Rev. Andrew Jensen and his family ... the worst disaster to hit the area in this century. The full extent of the tragedy is not yet known."

Sometimes, little things like making sure the center page of the bulletin is inserted, make a huge difference.

Leon Westerhouse was a music evangelist for fifty-four years. No full-time church position, no regular salary. Travel that never stopped. His family lived on the love offerings from churches and revivals. His goal was simple: tell everyone about Jesus. He referred to himself as "Leon the peon" or as "plain ol' Leon." No Brylcreem-basted hair or slick suits for him. The spotlight wasn't important. Winning souls was.

Leon's purpose was to share the Gospel. He went on mission trips to at least fifteen or twenty countries. Just one ten-day trip to Brazil that he participated in led to over 30,000 souls won for eternity. Little things make a huge difference. As a result of the decades of faithfully contributing through the little things he did, Leon Westerhouse was an inaugural inductee in the Evangelists' Hall of Faith.

Leon's most treasured verse was "In the same way, let your light shine before men, so that they may see your good works and give glory to your Father in heaven (Matthew 5:16 HCSB). He signed letters, "Keep shining for Jesus!"

Little things do make a huge difference. When Fred and Nancy Traynham's Air Force assignment took them to Germany, their land-lady helped Nancy learn the language by asking questions in German. One day she queried, "What did you cook for dinner?" Nancy meant to answer "Hähnchen," which means "chicken." Unfortunately, she actually replied, "Hündchen," which means "puppy."

The little things done by countless peons changes lives forever. The hands on our life clock are spinning crazily. They show it's time to get busy. Your little acts of service for God truly will make a huge difference. "Keep shining for Jesus!"

My most significant takeaways:

How I will apply this:

Other related scriptures:

46

Rebounds, Ricochets, and Ruh-Ro

Everyone has experienced their own "Ruh-ro" moments. (If you're unsure about the definition of "Ruh-ro," watch a few Scooby Doo reruns.) Some of our miscues are physical errors, while others fall into the "What was I thinking?" category.

Former employees of Avco Manufacturing told how, years ago, personnel were not required to clock out during lunch time. Strangely, a coworker did just that one day. They said he clocked out, went on lunch break, robbed a bank, then casually returned to work and clocked in. Laughing as they told the story, they concluded, "If he hadn't clocked out and back in, he would never have been caught for the bank robbery." Yep, some ruh-ros are mental. Then there are the others.

It was a beautiful 82-degree July afternoon, perfect for a round of golf. Dan Dawson and I stepped to the tee box for the thirteenth hole, a short 110-yard approach on the Nashboro Golf Club course. Dan teed up his ball, took a smooth backswing, and unleashed the coiled-up energy. The Titleist rocketed off the face of his nine-iron – toward a tree thirty yards down the right side of the fairway. Ruh-ro! The dimpled ball slammed into the trunk of a maple tree (no doubt putting a dimple on the unsuspecting maple) and rebounded on a bee-line straight toward Dan. The ricochet bounded up the front of the tee box on a direct line to my stunned playing partner. Without even moving his feet, he quickly bent over and snagged the fast-running ball as smoothly as a major league shortstop fields a hard-hit grounder. (Instead of being highlighted on the Golf Channel, some of our errant shots were best suited for "America's Funniest Videos.")

God's wisdom guides us in how to deal with the blunders that bounce back or even blow up. Let's begin with the fact that "People cannot see their own mistakes" (Psalm 19:12 NCV). Now add a personal admission to the mix: "We all make mistakes in all kinds of ways" (James 3:2 Phillips NT). Whether it is us or someone else, recovering from a ricochet truly is possible. "A man who refuses to admit his mistakes can never be successful. But if he confesses and forsakes them, he gets another chance" (Proverbs 28:13 TLB).

Oh, the incredible joy of giving – or getting – a second chance. Let's try to be just a little less demanding and instead be a lot more understanding when we, or those around us, have a ruh-ro moment. That act of compassion is much easier if we just follow the Lord's guidance. "Love forgets mistakes." (Proverbs 17:9 TLB)

Jesus has forgotten all of my mistakes. For all of eternity. Because of His love.

My most significant takeaways:

How I will apply this:

Other related scriptures:

47

Taking Care of Business

Elvis Presley firmly believed in his mantra, "Taking Care of Business," so much so that he chose that as his band's name. He wore both a necklace and a ring with "TCB" surrounding a lightning bolt, which signified taking care of business in a flash. But what if business isn't taken care of in a flash?

A friend named Terry leases a commercial property and operates his business there. An ongoing headache has been getting the landlord to make needed repairs in a timely manner. Repeated calls led to repeated promises that were repeatedly broken. Problems can only be ignored so long before they become far worse.

Recently a customer asked to use the restroom at Terry's business. The customer was just sitting there, minding his own business while taking care of business, when the toilet suddenly turned over and chucked him into the shower stall. Terry's brother, Gene, commented, "The toilet is supposed to be facing east-west, but now it's headed due north!" Fear of a possible lawsuit caused priorities to be shifted for the landlord as quickly as the ceramic stool shifted under the customer.

The King delivered a powerful Time Management seminar to his disciples when He said, "But seek first the kingdom of God and His righteousness, and all these things will be provided for you" (Matthew 6:33 HCSB). Prioritize, He said. Take care of business. Seek first, before you worry about your career. Seek first, before you get wrapped up in vacation plans. Take care of business before hobbies, shopping, or another degree. Seek first. Everything else will be provided.

God knows how our priorities sometimes get out of whack. USA Today ran an article on October 25th, 1995 that read, "Ronald Warwick, captain of the luxury cruise ship Queen Elizabeth II, questioned a passenger who paid full fare for his dog to join them on an around-the-world cruise. (Accommodations ranged from $25,000 to $150,000.) 'Wouldn't it have cost less to leave him at home?' "'Oh no,' the man said.' When we are away a long time, the dog's psychiatrist fees are so high, it's less expensive to bring him along!'"

Seek first, and then "Rejoice always! Pray constantly. Give thanks in everything, for this is God's will for you in Christ Jesus" (1 Thess. 5:16-18)

Ancient church father Augustine of Hippo once said, "Christ is not valued at all, unless he is valued above all." A Christian's real priority summed up in a dozen words. Our life is but a flash. It is time for us to be taking care of business.

My most significant takeaways:

How I will apply this:

Other related scriptures:

48

The More You Get, the More You Want

Everyone has had some material item, outside of basic needs, that they wished for. I was certainly no exception. Growing up during Detroit's muscle-car era gave me a great love for fast, sleek vehicles. It was the heyday of Mustang, GTO, Chevelle, Charger, Olds 442, Camaro, and more of those high-octane beauties.

With that appreciation of powerful cars, I finally bought a brand new Chevy Nova. It looked fast. Sadly, it was more meek than muscle. Fueled by that disappointment, I went looking for a trade. And there it sat! Glistening black with gold pin striping, wide tires, and a reputation that had captured America's attention – the famous Pontiac Firebird Trans Am. This car's popularity had skyrocketed due to the "Smokey and the Bandit" movies, and this one beckoned me alluringly. The salesman asked if I wanted to test drive it. Does a starving man want a steak?

He handed me the key and I slid behind the wheel. Bucket seats. Four in the floor transmission. New car smell. This was truly car heaven! The massive engine roared to life, and we turned toward the street.

And before I could pull off the dealer's lot, the mighty Trans Am ran out of gas.

Talk about someone popping your balloon! Romans 8:28 (HCSB) authoritatively proclaims, "We know that all things work together for the good of those who love God," but as the 400 cubic inch engine spit and sputtered and died, there didn't seem to be any way this situation was working for my good. The Trans Am coasted to a stop and my dream of replacing Burt Reynolds as the king of cool, vaporized. Thankfully, I now see that another scripture would have served me far better, both at that moment and for the rest of my life: "Take delight in the LORD, and He will give you your heart's desires" (Psalm 37:4 HCSB).

Part of our earthly nature is an unquenchable thirst for things, whether or not they are actually needed. That affliction seems to start very early in life, proven by one couple's story. They said, "We were very proud of our nearly two-year-old son who was learning to say 'please' and 'thank you.' After he opened various gifts from friends at Christmas, we asked him, 'Zachary, what do you say to Diana and Alejandra?' Zachary smiled and responded, 'More, please.'"

"Set your minds on what is above, not on what is on the earth" (Colossians 3:2).

My most significant takeaways:

How I will apply this:

Other related scriptures:

49

A Change of Heart

There is one word in the English language that brings either great joy or great fear. Anticipation or dread. Love or hate. What single word can be so divisive and so polarizing? That word is "change."

The concept of New Year's resolutions suggests we should commit to some changes or improvements in our life. The dawn of a new year offers a time of reflection. Eat more healthily. Handle money more wisely. Exercise less frequently (my wife, Lynn, suggests that one each year!). Maybe we could consider adding "Keep out of trouble" to the list of changes.

Matt Coleman was like most seven-year-old boys. Active, inquisitive, and adventurous. And as you might expect, trouble regularly found its way to him. After one episode where Matt's mischief caught up to him, his mother delivered a dose of corrective parental medicine. Then, like generations of parents before her, with hands on hips Gail sternly demanded, "WHY did you do that?"

That's a tough question when you are seven. Will any answer calm this storm? Matt pondered her query for a moment, then pulled himself up to his full forty-nine inch height and firmly answered, "A man's got to do what a man's got to do."

What is it that you have "got to do" this next year? Jesus said, "You are my friends if you do what I command you (John 15:14)." Maybe becoming more obedient to the Lord's commands is a wonderful starting point.

Scripture offers a multi-pronged planning guide to assist us during the upcoming twelve months: "It is evident who are the children of God. The Lord's servant must not be quarrelsome but kind to everyone. Avoid foolish controversies. The one who searches for what is good finds favor. Through love serve one another. (1 John 3:10 ESV; 2 Timothy 2:24; Titus 3:9; Proverbs 11:27 HCSB; Galatians 5:13 ESV)

As committed believers, we need to surrender to the changes the Spirit wants to work within us. Some kids, though, try to negotiate with God about changing.

One little boy was overheard praying: "Lord, if you can't make me a better boy, don't worry about it. I'm having a real good time like I am."

Look forward to the changes and the blessings they bring. Happy New Year!

My most significant takeaways:

How I will apply this:

Other related scriptures:

50

A Helping Hand and Hot Water

It was four a.m. Thermometers shivered in the bitterly-cold three degrees. Marvin Estes had stopped at a convenience store on Dickerson Road to restock the supply of the weekly "Wheels and Deals" publication. This particular part of Nashville has a long-standing reputation as an area where women and men, shall we say, connect at nighttime. Before Marvin could leave the store, a woman approached and asked for a ride to the Krystal restaurant a few blocks away. Marvin is a big guy with a big heart, so he naturally said yes. Speaking of that fateful morning, he says, "It was three degrees outside. I thought I could help her a little bit."

Marvin's truck had barely begun moving when the woman unexpectedly propositioned him, which was the last thing on his mind since he was on his way to meet his wife. Her business offer had barely stopped echoing in the cab of his truck when blue lights flashed right behind him. A sickening sense of dread engulfed Marvin as he pulled off the street. He knew he was in hot water. The officers accused him of solicitation. And his Good Samaritan explanation? It was met with a combination of laughter and disbelief.

False accusations rip through lives like an F5 tornado. Unfounded charges can destroy your family, reputation, or witness. As you hang on tightly while the tempests buffet you mercilessly, hold on to this promise from God: "Consider it a sheer gift, friends, when tests and challenges come at you from all sides.

You know that under pressure, your faith-life is forced into the open and shows its true colors. No weapon turned against you shall succeed, and you will have justice against every courtroom lie. This is the heritage of the servants of the Lord" (James 1:2-3 MSG; Isaiah 54:17 TLB).

If you get into trouble for helping somebody, know that you are in good company. Jesus was frequently in hot water with the religious elites for giving a helping hand. Healing a man's withered hand on the Sabbath. Allowing his hungry disciples to eat grain from a field. Dining with sinners and tax collectors.

The police finally believed Marvin Estes's story and released him. No mug shot on the six-o'clock news! Like him, you may be accused falsely for offering a bit of aid. The reward is definitely worth the risk. John Bunyan, author of the Christian allegory *The Pilgrim's Progress*, noted, "You have not lived today until you have done something for someone who can never repay you."

Ignore the rising temperature. Do something for someone. Offer a helping hand.

My most significant takeaways:

How I will apply this:

Other related scriptures:

51

The Sky Is Falling

Remember the story of Chicken Little, who proclaimed, "The sky is falling!?" Arthur Shaffer can relate. His mother told him a story from his early childhood, a story that was confirmed years later by the editor of the Grayson (KY) Journal Enquirer. Two-year-old Arthur was sitting in his high chair as his mother fed him when the not yet potty-trained Arthur's number two suddenly became his number one priority. The feeding was put on hold as his mother took him to the bathroom for an impromptu cleanup. At that same moment, a construction crew was excavating for a new road nearby. They set off a dynamite charge that launched a boulder sixteen inches in diameter skyward, a rock that returned to earth by crashing through the roof of the Shaffer's kitchen. This projectile from the sky scored a direct hit on the high chair and reduced it to a pile of splinters.

Four years later Arthur was sitting in his first grade class when someone dropped a book onto the floor of the classroom directly above, causing the entire plaster ceiling in Mrs. Wolford's classroom to turn loose and fall onto Arthur and his terrified classmates. Like a scene from the Three Stooges, some students actually had a doughnut-shaped section of plaster surrounding their head as it came to rest on their shoulders. The sky is falling!

Wait a minute, you say. Aren't Christians supposed to be shielded? Well...no. The great apostle and missionary Paul rightly observed, "We can rejoice, too, when we run into problems and trials, for we know that they help us develop endurance. And endurance develops strength of character, and character strengthens our confident hope of salvation. And this hope will not lead to disappointment. For we know how dearly God loves us, because he has given us the Holy Spirit to fill our hearts with his love." (Romans 5:3-5 NLT)

There is no way to anticipate when or how the sky will start falling. A preacher was well into his sermon when he noticed his young son standing in the balcony, throwing balls of paper onto the heads of people in the congregation. The pastor was just about to command his son to stop when the boy called out encouragingly, "Don't worry, Dad. You just keep preaching and I'll keep them awake!"

In every situation, whatever comes at you out of the clear blue, "Rejoice in hope, be patient in tribulation, be constant in prayer." (Romans 12:12)

My most significant takeaways:

How I will apply this:

Other related scriptures:

52

Knowing Job One

In 1981 Ford Motor Company introduced a new advertising tagline: "Quality is Job One." Ford used that slogan for seventeen years in an effort to overcome their negative reputation as a manufacturer of rust buckets. Other companies would be well-served by determining what is truly most important. One accounting firm's misguided list of values placed their profit at number one and their people at number four.

A young boy by the name of James had a desire to be the most famous manufacturer and salesman of cheese in the world. He planned on becoming rich and famous by making and selling cheese and began with a little buggy pulled by a pony named Paddy. After making his cheese, he would load his wagon and he and Paddy would drive down the streets of Chicago to sell the cheese. As the months passed, the young boy began to despair because he was not making any money, in spite of his long hours and hard work.

One day he pulled his pony to a stop and began to talk to him. He said, "Paddy, there is something wrong. We are not doing it right. I am afraid we have things turned around and our priorities are not where they ought to be. Maybe we ought to serve God and place Him first in our lives." The boy drove home and made a covenant that for the rest of his life he would first serve God and then would work as God directed.

Many years after this, the young boy, now a man, stood as Sunday School Superintendent at North Shore Baptist Church in Chicago and said, "I would rather be a layman in the North Shore Baptist Church than to head the greatest corporation in America. My first job is serving Jesus."

So, every time you take a take a bite of Philadelphia Cream cheese, sip a cup of Maxwell House, mix a quart of Kool-Aid, slice up a DiGiorno Pizza, cook a pot of Macaroni & Cheese, spread some Grey Poupon, stir a bowl of Cream of Wheat, slurp down some Jell-O, eat the cream out of the middle of an Oreo cookie, or serve some Stove Top Stuffing, remember a boy, his pony named Paddy, and the promise little James L. Kraft made to serve God and work as He directed.

The prophet Samuel's direction concerning service still rings true today: "Fear the Lord and serve him faithfully with all your heart. For consider what great things he has done for you" (1 Samuel 12:24 ESV). Fear the Lord, and serve him faithfully. Make no mistake about it: this is Job One for every believer.

My most significant takeaways:

How I will apply this:

Other related scriptures:

53

Paying Up For Paying Back

Wintertime in 1962 at Prichard School in Grayson, KY, meant someone had to carry the coal for the fourth-grade classroom. A single pot-bellied stove kept the students moderately comfortable, but the ravenous beast had an appetite that was never satisfied. Mrs. Stringer seemed to choose one student more than frequently than anyone else for the dirty and unenviable task – Oscar McGinnis.

If you have ever felt singled out or picked on, then you can understand how Oscar viewed this situation. The more often Mrs. Stringer handed him this onerous job, the more his resentment built. Then one evening at home, Oscar found a pack of firecrackers and immediately concocted a plan to get back at his unfair teacher.

The next day, as Oscar finished loading the coal into the stove, he casually dropped the pack of firecrackers into the building inferno. His clandestine mission complete, Oscar dutifully returned to his seat and waited – and waited – and waited some more. He now says, "I thought those firecrackers were never going to go off!" Just as he had given up hope...BOOM!!!! The thunderous explosion almost ripped the eight-inch steel exhaust pipe off the stove.

Mrs. Stringer immediately knew what had happened. She snatched the long, heavy switch off the top of the chalkboard and marched back to Oscar's desk. Oscar said, "She wore me out right beside my desk. The worst part was, I got even more coal duty!" Author Robert Louis Stevenson noted, "Sooner or later, everyone sits down to a banquet of consequences." Oscar's escapade definitely brought consequences as his "sits down" part was rather tender for some time.

The Bible directly contradicts our desire for revenge, saying, "But to you who are listening I say: Love your enemies, do good to those who hate you, bless those who curse you, pray for those who mistreat you. (Luke 6:27-28 NLT)

Letting go of the emotions that drive our impulse to get someone back is hard, even for believers. A little boy was smarting after being punished by his father. Shortly afterward, he knelt by his bed to say prayers, which ended with the usual blessings for all the family members but one. Then he turned to his father and said, "I suppose you noticed you weren't in it."

The best approach to dealing with offenses, real or imagined, is to just follow God's directives: "Hatred stirs up conflicts, but love covers all offenses. Love your neighbor as yourself." (Proverbs 10:12; Leviticus 19:18 HCSB)

My most significant takeaways:

How I will apply this:

Other related scriptures:

54

Scared Silly

When Karla Burnett was five years old, her family had an outing to Kentucky Lake. Staying in a somewhat primitive cabin meant there were no indoor facilities, which wasn't too bad – during the daytime. The story changed dramatically after dark. Who knows what wild or ferocious animals are lurking in the inky black of the night? Still, when a little girl has to go, the call of nature will not be denied.

Karla's mother dutifully took her outdoors, but only part of the way to the outhouse. The long journey was magnified by their fear of the unknown. Mom had Karla stop midway of the trek and instructed her to take care of business right there. Since Mom knows best, and since Karla didn't really want to walk all the way to the outhouse in the pitch-black gloom, this seemed like a really good idea.

Karla squatted down, nervously looking around for the monstrous beasts that were ready to devour a little girl like her. She had been close to the ground for scant seconds when a giant creature ran under her backside and right between her legs! Karla screamed and toppled over! Mom screamed and ran back to the cabin! Poor, traumatized Karla was left behind in the scary darkness to face the predator alone.

As she crawled to her knees, Karla noticed the vicious creature a few feet away. But instead of some unearthly being with glowing red eyes, gigantic fangs, and bad breath, she saw a small, furry critter that had long, tall ears and a fluffy cottontail.

Maybe you have been scared silly at some point in your life. The upcoming rent or mortgage payment. The diagnosis after a battery of tests. Facing your family after an ugly and long separation. Admittedly, even Christians deal with concerns that leave them shaking in their boots, but that need not be the case.

Thankfully, our God wants us to trust instead of tremble when life seems fearful. First, know that you are not alone as you walk through the dark. Scripture tells us, "He will be with you; he will not leave you or forsake you. Do not fear or be dismayed." (Deut. 31:8 ESV) Then the Lord offers His calming voice, saying, "Don't be afraid, I've redeemed you. I've called your name. You're mine. For those who love God all things work together for good. (Isaiah 43:1; Romans 8:28).

Fear not. When you trust in Him, lions become lambs and werewolves turn into wabbits.

My most significant takeaways:

How I will apply this:

Other related scriptures:

55

Blaze of Glory

The chorus of Kenny Rogers' 1981 hit song, Blaze of Glory, concludes with the lines, "Let's go out like we came in; In a blaze of glory." These phrases offer a tip of the hat to the western movies and television shows where one or more characters, when facing insurmountable odds, elected to make one last fateful charge and go down with six-shooters blazing. For those of us who have collected a few extra decades, our day-to-day lives reveal that we are often going out, not in a blaze of glory, but in a flicker of hilarious missteps.

A high school classmate named Martha Jordan recently posted a comment about her husband on Facebook: "Well, John brushed his teeth with Icy Hot. The sad thing is that it's not the first time he's done that!! We're both so pitiful – lol."

Valna Goodwin once told me how she and her husband, Estill, were in a gospel quartet with another couple. They had been practicing for hours but were not quite finished. When the other lady opened her mouth and started the next song, her false teeth launched out of her mouth and went flying halfway across the room.

The prophet Daniel found himself in a life-or-death situation when King Darius was deceived and signed an order declaring no one could pray to any god for 30 days. Violation of this irrevocable law required the offender immediately be thrown into the lion's den. Decision time was at hand. Obey the laws of the kingdom or continue praying to Jehovah? Cower in darkness or go out in a blaze of glory? We discover his answer in Daniel 6:10 HCSB – "When Daniel learned that the document had been signed, he went into his house. The windows in its upper room opened toward Jerusalem, and three times a day he got down on his knees, prayed, and gave thanks to his God, just as he had done before."

Daniel's lion-hearted approach to possible death and his protection by an angel caused King Darius to write every nation on earth, saying, "People must tremble in fear before the God of Daniel: For He is the living God, and He endures forever." (verse 26) Yes, Icy Hot and denture cream might be some of your dearest friends now. Whether or not that is the case, pray and thank our Father for another day and for another opportunity to go out in a blaze of glory – for Him.

My most significant takeaways:

How I will apply this:

Other related scriptures:

56

Jumping To Conclusions

You have probably heard the humorous saying, "If it looks like a duck, swims like a duck, and quacks like a duck, then it probably is a duck." The key word in that phrase is "probably." Probably doesn't mean definitively, certainly, or absolutely. It means likely.

Glenda and Mark were heroin addicts. After leaving the government-sponsored clinic where they were given methadone as part of their rehab process, they were involved in a very serious car crash that left both of them hospitalized for several days.

When Glenda asked for her purse as she was being discharged, the staff informed her that her personal belongings were at the police station. That response puzzled her, so naturally her next stop was at the Grant Police Department on Grant Mountain, Alabama.

Glenda asked for her possessions, and a Barney Fife-like officer curtly responded (imagine a high-pitched, nasal voice), "You can have your purse back – just as soon as you tell us what the white powder is in that zip-lock bag inside your purse!" (Can't you picture him using his pinky finger to dab in the dust and then tasting it, like in the movies?)

Shocked beyond belief, Glenda shouted, "The powder? In the plastic bag in my purse? That's my mother's ashes!!!"

Jumping to conclusions can be embarrassing at the least and extremely costly if someone decides to sue over the situation. We find a well-advised caution in Proverbs 25:8, which reads "Don't jump to conclusions - there may be a perfectly good explanation for what you just saw."

It is easy to make the leap. A church leader was driving the car in front of you, and you watched him turn on the street that leads to the bad part of town. "And just what is he doing going over there?" you accusingly wonder. The answer comes on Sunday when the pastor reads a thank-you note from the family of a soldier killed in battle – a family who lives in the bad part of town. A family in need. A family he had gone to console.

Be careful about jumping to conclusions. Wait for more information to arrive.

After all, some ugly ducklings turn into beautiful swans.

My most significant takeaways:

How I will apply this:

Other related scriptures:

57

The Power of Words

Lily and Honey were sisters who lived in a big house at the intersection of Eastland Avenue and Gallatin Road in East Nashville. These elderly spinsters were known to have significant money, and the lure was too much for a couple of guys who decided to break in late one evening.

The gray-haired gals heard the commotion at the back door as the robbers attempted to force their way in. These senior citizen sisters had never owned a gun in their lives, much less shot one, but when they heard the vandals, Lily yelled loudly, "Honey, get your gun!!! Shoot them! Shoot them through the door! Honey, get your gun and shoot them!!"

Upon hearing those words, the robbers became runners. They probably thought the woman was calling for a man, "Honey," and being broke was far better than being blasted with buckshot. They never heard a pump shotgun being racked, but the words they heard caused them to anticipate bullets flying through the door at any second. The words achieved Lily's desired result.

Words are powerful. They can be used as a blade or a bandage. Proverbs 12:18 advises, "There is one whose rash words are like sword thrusts, but the tongue of the wise brings healing."

Proverbs 18:21 cautions, "Death and life are in the power of the tongue." (It's really true – the robbers ran for their lives because of Lily's words!) Relationships are either built or destroyed – by words. Doors may be opened or slammed shut – by words. Criticism or comfort can be conveyed – by words.

If you are like most people, there are some words you wish you could unspeak, simply because of the hurt and tears they caused. Do your best to fix the future. Choose now to pause and consider the power of your words before unleashing them.

After all, if you have been giving someone the devil, it makes it awfully hard to tell them about Christ.

My most significant takeaways:

How I will apply this:

Other related scriptures:

58

Somebody Save Me

Nashville's 2024 unexpected snowfall of 6.5 inches took me on a trip and sent me skiing down memory lane to fifty years earlier. It was surprisingly cold the morning of Friday, February 9, 1973 at Robins Air Force Base, Georgia. Much colder than the typical winter days in middle Georgia. The greater surprise rolled in at about 0830 when the slate-gray sky began to overflow. Large, heavy, wet snowflakes fell in rapid succession. They began to huddle together and then invited their family and friends to join them. When the party finally ended Saturday morning, a New England-like sixteen-inch snowfall blanketed the area.

The National Weather Service dubbed the event "The Great Southeastern Snowstorm." The icy intrusion locked down I-75 from Chattanooga all the way into north Florida, leaving many motorists stranded with little or no food, fuel, or protection from the frigid conditions. When people are in jeopardy, they need someone to ride to the rescue. Airmen from the base were quickly dispatched on their trusty steeds (deuce and a half trucks) to save those scared travelers.

At some point, everyone needs help. It isn't just the proverbial "damsel in distress." It could be the rich and powerful. The poor and downtrodden. Average Janes and Joes going about their average activities. And then, suddenly, a giant snowball of trouble comes barreling down the mountain right toward them.

We can be thankful many have been brought to emotional or physical or financial safety because someone responded when they saw a person in dire need. Daring rescues form the plot lines of novels, movies, television shows, and real life situations. Maybe that inspiration comes from the Lord God, who has been in the business of rescuing people for quite some time.

The Israelites were slaves in Egypt; Yahweh sent Moses. His children were without food or water; Jehovah Jireh provided nourishment. Two spies sent by Joshua into Jericho were saved by Rahab. The Persian king's unwitting decree threatened the lives of every Jewish person; God had Esther in place to plead for their safety. The people of Nineveh needed God's compassionate love, so He sent Jonah (who took the scenic route before finally fulfilling his commission).

The most amazing and incredible story is when Jesus rescued you and me. For others, He stands ready, simply waiting to hear their request: "LORD, I seek refuge in You;... In Your justice, rescue and deliver me." (Psalm 71:1-2 HCSB)

My most significant takeaways:

How I will apply this:

Other related scriptures:

59

Getting Into Hot Water

Most baptisms are a mixture of somberness and celebration. Most. And then there are the others. Many pastors have great stories of the bobbles, bungles, and boo-boos that were central to some of their most memorable baptisms.

Even during this very religious moment, humanity can take hold of people. In his book, "The Preacher," Tommy Cunningham breaks out some of his funniest baptism experiences. You will enjoy his description of one particular event.

"'It was a winter night and quite cold outside the little Southern Baptist church. My helper had turned on the water heater several hours earlier so the water would be heated adequately. For some reason, the heater malfunctioned and failed to cycle correctly. The water was just short of boiling when I stepped into the baptistry. I could tell it was unusually hot, even though I was wearing insulated chest waders.

The middle-aged lady entered the water and looked somewhat stressed. Her face became bright red with splotches breaking out on her neck. She walked carefully up to the front of the baptistry when the curtains opened. At that point her old, sinful nature took over and she exclaimed, "Oh, ---- this water is hot!"

It surely wasn't the Holy Spirit that fell on the worshipers that night. It was a single giggle that started in the back and eventually filled the entire auditorium. She turned to me and said, "Oh, Brother Tommy, I'm so sorry that word just slipped out." I replied, "Hold your breath, sister, you need this baptism worse than I thought!'"

If you wonder why people fight this battle, Galatians 5:17 (AMP) provides the answer: "For the sinful nature has its desire which is opposed to the Spirit, and the desire of the Spirit opposes the sinful nature; for these two, (the sinful nature and the Spirit) are in direct opposition to each other, so that you (as believers) do not (always) do whatever (good things) you want to do."

Our sinful nature gets us into hot water. Depend upon the Spirit to help you keep your cool.

My most significant takeaways:

How I will apply this:

Other related scriptures:

60

Never Fear

L.C. McCoy laughs heartily now as he tells this story on him-self. Two employees had not shown up for work that particular day, leaving him with a large task where he really needed assistance. Upset over their irresponsibility, L.C. was preoccupied with his anger as he stepped from the bright sunlight into the darkness of the unoccupied portable classroom (where the teacher also instructed Tae Kwon Do) at Mt. View Elementary School. He had barely stormed past the doorway when he glanced to his left and saw the silhouette of a man standing across the room. Unaware the teacher had brought a practice dummy to class, L.C. instantly thought someone had broken into the classroom. Out the door he flew!

After getting only two steps outside, L.C. felt a sharp, searing pain in the back of his neck. "He shot me!" was his immediate thought, believing the "intruder" was out for the kill. The burning pain, though, did not come from a bullet. L.C. had been nailed by a ticked-off wasp that got stirred up when he threw the door open.

Fear and pain can be troublesome. Fear began in the Garden of Eden with the fall of mankind. Fear might be momentary, misplaced, or a bona fide reason for a "Mayday" call of distress. The Psalmist in 118:6 offers help by saying, "The Lord is for me; I will not be afraid. What can man do to me?" We should memorize and then recall these comforting words frequently, especially when difficulties are looming or, like L.C., we find ourselves panicked by something.

Pain is also present in our lives, like a smudge on an otherwise-beautiful painting. Our heavenly Father wants to safeguard and protect us, but pain is part of the consequence we suffer because of Adam's and Eve's fruit pie indulgence. Pain, though, is much more bearable when put into the right perspective, as seen in Romans 8:18 – "For I consider that the sufferings of this present time are not worth comparing with the glory that is going to be revealed to us."

Admittedly, fear can be a pain in the neck. The Lord asks us to focus on Him instead of on shadowy figures. Best of all, while we might get hit by a wasp, trusting in God ensures we never will never experience the sting of eternal death.

My most significant takeaways:

How I will apply this:

Other related scriptures:

61

A Matter of Respect

Rodney Dangerfield became famous for his comedy routine based upon his catchphrase, "I don't get no respect."

All of us get that. We understand that feeling. Unfortunately, the concept of not getting respect was painfully reinforced for me just last week.

While golfing is enjoyable for me, any average golfer has skills that far outshine my own. I recognize that shortcoming and readily admit to it – without harassment or nasty reminders from critics.

I was hitting a few golf balls during a practice session last week when a Springer Spaniel from a nearby home came bounding toward me, spun around quickly, and made a beeline for my golf bag. This beautiful dog must have had a heart of stone. He stopped, stared defiantly at me, hiked his leg, and peed on my golf bag as if to say, "Here is what I think of your golf game!"

It is really sad when even an animal is dogging you! I don't get no respect!

Even though Christians may live in a dog-eat-dog world, our goal is to live in a manner that brings honor to God. Our approach should be different than the critics that swarm around us like irritating gnats. Romans 12:10 points us toward a higher road when it says, "Be devoted to each other like a loving family. Excel in showing respect for each other."

Albert Einstein's take on respect is notable and commendable: *"I speak to everyone in the same way, whether he is the garbage man or the president of the university."* Whether it is someone's golf game, political viewpoint, religious belief, or something else we perceive as a shortcoming, just remember: people may not remember the words you say, but they will remember how you made them feel.

Make your Father proud! Excel in showing respect for each other.

My most significant takeaways:

How I will apply this:

Other related scriptures:

62

Your Own Free Will

Rev. Martha Rucker is a chaplain at St. Thomas Hospital in Nashville, and I had the occasion to meet her recently during an interview process. She commented, "In looking over your biography, I see that you are from Grayson, Kentucky. Not many people know where Grayson is, let alone have lived there, and I did – for seven years." We spent the next several minutes connecting the dots between people both of us knew. Martha laughed as she added, "Not long after we moved there, my husband, Dennis, went uptown to The Frame Shop to, obviously, get something framed. He mentioned to the owner that he had just moved to Grayson.

The owner looked at Dennis uncertainly and asked, 'Are you in the witness protection program? Nobody moves to Grayson of their own free will!'"

When it comes to choosing where to serve the Lord, our inclination might be somewhere exotic, like Hawaii. A star-studded locale, such as New York City or Los Angeles. Someplace comfortable, perhaps even where you grew up. After all, why would anyone go to Africa, Alaska, or the Amazon jungle? Why opt for Cleveland, China, or Cambodia? Why would anyone move to Guatemala, Ghana, or Grayson of their own free will? Why? The answer lies in a single word – trust.

Have I not commanded you? Be strong and courageous. Do not be frightened, and do not be dismayed, for the Lord your God is with you wherever you go. For God gave us a spirit not of fear but of power and love and self-control. You did not choose me, but I chose you and appointed you that you should go and bear fruit and that your fruit should abide. Trust in the Lord with all your heart, and do not lean on your own understanding. (Joshua 1:9; 2 Timothy 1:7; John 15:16; Proverbs 3:5 ESV)

Staying in our comfort zone is easy. It can also be disobedient. Maybe you haven't been asked to lead a nation out of slavery. How about leading one person out of the slavery of sin? No assignment to do something huge like building an ark? Maybe you could help someone rebuild their life. You don't have to walk on water. Just walk across the street and earnestly share your heart and God's love.

Drive a stake in the lawn and put up the "Moving" sign. Pack up and get ready to leave your safe place. Isn't it about time to trust and go – of your own free will?

My most significant takeaways:

How I will apply this:

Other related scriptures:

63

Being In the Dark

Change. Some people love it. Adapt easily. It is a breeze! For others, it's tough. Rapid change can leave you in the dark. New things can be challenging. And sometimes downright embarrassing.

Mary Enander is a friend of several years, and her recent Facebook post was certainly attention-getting, as well as downright funny. She said, "I love my husband. In many ways he isn't, but in many other ways he's an innocent soul. (Her way of saying he is totally clueless about some things!) Now we have moved into the digital age, and our plane tickets are on our phone. To have these plane tickets read, you simply place the phone screen face down near a scanner, much like in a grocery store.

Unfortunately, my husband got to the security scanner before me. A very nice security guard, whose year my husband just made, told him, "Face down, please."

So my husband, G. Erik Enander, literally puts his face down to the scanner, much to the delight of the TSA officers.

Don't worry, they helped my 'very special husband' through the process, and he finally understood. I am proud to say that he laughed at himself perhaps even more than the guards."

God's plan has never been for His chosen people to be confused or in the dark. Just the opposite. "In the beginning God created the heavens and the earth. Then God said, "Let there be light," and there was light." (Genesis 1:1,3 HCSB) (No need to create man first and have him stumbling in the darkness!)

Even though the plague of darkness covered Egypt, "all the Israelites had light where they lived." (Exodus 10:23) The ultimate light, the life-saving light, given by God was His son. "Then Jesus spoke to them again: "I am the light of the world. Anyone who follows Me will never walk in the darkness but will have the light of life." (John 8:12)

Face it, some changes may leave us totally in the dark. When it comes to eternity, though, God has clearly illuminated the pathway that leads to heaven.

My most significant takeaways:

How I will apply this:

Other related scriptures:

64

Last Words

Obituaries offer limited space to capture the essence of a person's life. Bob Hoover passed away on October 25, 2016, and the obituary of the 94-year-old Nashville native could have filled pages – or volumes. Bob was known throughout the aviation world for his great record of testing supersonic jets and demonstrating unmatched skill as a stunt performer in a myriad of aircraft. For example, while flying a Russian aircraft at a Russian air show, Hoover thoroughly outshone the Soviet pilots. The embarrassed home country held Bob in custody before his friend, Russian Cosmonaut Yuri Gagarin, intervened and secured his release.

Bob enlisted in the Tennessee National Guard and was a fighter pilot during WWII. On his fifty-ninth mission, he was captured after his malfunctioning Spitfire was shot down by the Luftwaffe. After spending sixteen months in Stalag Luft I, Hoover and a friend escaped the prison camp, then stole a German aircraft and flew it to the Netherlands. When you consider a summary of one's life, Bob Hoover's obituary reveals a man of tremendous skill, courage, and resolve.

Let's compare Bob's story with this account from a New Orleans parish deputy. A few years earlier he and his partner responded to a call for a possible breaking and entering. As they cautiously crept toward the house, this deputy drew his pistol. He then looked over his shoulder to communicate instructions to his partner – and was stunned to see him standing there empty-handed. "Where is your gun?" the deputy angrily whispered. His partner sheepishly mumbled, "I forgot it at home."

Whatever our task, preparation is key. Former Marine Buddy Kidd told me the "Five Ps" axiom he learned in boot camp: Prior preparation prevents poor performance. The Lord offers guidance for those who would perform well in His service: "Sow with a view to righteousness, Reap in accordance with kindness; Break up your fallow ground, For it is time to seek the LORD Until He comes to rain righteousness on you." (Hosea 10:12 NASB) Be prepared. Have a focused purpose. Then get busy. Your rewards will come later.

Bob Hoover's preparedness led him to enshrinement in the National Aviation Hall of Fame. The deputy's lack of preparedness could have landed him in the Police Hall of Shame. Jesus directed, "Be dressed in readiness, and keep your lamps lit." May the last words about your life reflect the light you brought to the world.

My most significant takeaways:

How I will apply this:

Other related scriptures:

65

Fulfilling His Trust

The drive through Rocky Mountain National Park had been spectacular. Lynn and I began our day-long journey in Estes Park and wound our way through the majestic mountains, stopping frequently to soak in the beauty and wonder of a small part of God's magnificent creation. We had not planned an agenda, so late afternoon found us at Grand Lake, Colorado. We scouted around for available rooms and soon discovered a small group of log cabins not far from the center of town. I called the number listed on the sign, and a most helpful lady pleasantly answered each of my questions. The surprise came when I asked if we could take a look inside a cabin before deciding, and she responded, "Sure thing. Just go on in. The door is unlocked."

Finding an owner who leaves the doors unlocked to her vacant rental units was shocking enough, especially in a tourist town, but she wasn't finished. The cabin was cozy and welcoming, so I called her again to reserve the unit and to ask about how to pay for the rental. This total stranger replied, "Oh, just leave a check on the kitchen table when you leave in the morning." Do what? I couldn't believe what I just heard!

Like this business owner trusted me, God trusts us. Sometimes His trust is justified; at other times, we fail miserably. Jesus gave the perfect example of that scenario in the Parable of the Talents. A businessman gave talents (money) to each of three men with the expectation they would put the money to work and earn him a profit. When the businessman returned some time later, one man had done very well with the money, another had done moderately well, and the third had simply buried the money for fear of losing the original investment. The two obedient men were praised by the owner, who said to each one, "Well done, good and faithful servant." (Matthew 25:21, 23 ESV) Disappointed and angry with the third man, the owner called him a "wicked and slothful servant!" (Matthew 25:26 ESV)

You and I have been equipped with talents and skills that are unique to us, and our Father trusts us to use them. The return on investment can be measured – by how many times you minister to someone in need or how many people you tell about Jesus. The Lord has unlocked the door to heaven for mankind. Let's choose to be worthy of the trust He has placed in us.

My most significant takeaways:

How I will apply this:

Other related scriptures:

66

What's Your Name Worth?

Joe McKeever of New Orleans is both a pastor and a very accomplished cartoonist. Joe was at Shocco Springs Baptist Conference Center in Talladega, AL, to draw pictures of the 700 attendees of the Foster Parents Conference. After sketching one young lad, Joe asked his name so he could add it to the drawing. The boy's reply was rather unclear, and when Joe asked him to repeat it, his older sister carefully spelled the name for Joe.

"P-h-u-r-i-o-u-s-l-y. Phuriously," she stated. "Seriously?" a dumbfounded Joe blurted out, thinking she was playing with him. "Yes," she said, "but we usually just call him Phury." Unable to contain himself, Joe had to ask, "And is your name Phast?" (Joe was slyly referencing the movie series, The Fast and the Furious.)

Names are unique and powerful. They can carry weight and influence – think of Kennedy, Rockefeller, or Vanderbilt. Names connect us to the past, and sometimes a single name is sufficient. Goliath, Hitler, Dracula, and Nero are some of history's most infamous figures. The names of Churchill, Lincoln, and Ghandi remind us of highly effective leaders. The realm of entertainment might offer Elvis, Disney, or Seuss. And of course, there is the wonderful name of Jesus.

What about your name? Proverbs 22:1 clearly states, "A good name is to be chosen rather than great riches." In other words, it isn't good for the local police officers to know you by name. Ecclesiastes 7:1 continues in the same vein, adding, "A good name is better than precious ointment."

After former Senator and U.S. Ambassador Howard Baker passed away, one of his close friends shared a wonderful story about Baker. Several years after retiring, Senator Baker went for an interview and took his grandson along. The interviewer referenced some of Baker's many accomplishments, and on the way home, his grandson looked at Baker and asked with wide-eyed amazement, "PawPaw, did you used to be somebody?"

You are much more than a Steady Eddie or a Plain Jane. Choose to be somebody. Let your good name be your calling card and your contribution to history.

My most significant takeaways:

How I will apply this:

Other related scriptures:

67

Opportunity Knocks

Bob Eubanks was the long-term host of the television show "The Newlywed Game," as well as a successful concert promoter and manager for some very notable country music acts such as Merle Haggard and Marty Robbins. Always searching for new talent to sign, Bob heard an Australian performer named Paul that he was convinced was going to be the next big splash in the music world.

Bob contacted Paul's manager in Australia and floated the idea of becoming his manager and expanding Paul's career. The manager was open to the possibility, under one condition. To sign Paul, Bob would also have to sign a young, blonde female singer the manager represented. Bob pushed back, saying, "Look, I already manage Dolly Parton and Barbara Mandrell. I have enough blondes to deal with as it is, so if that is the only way, then forget it." Later, Bob wistfully recalled, "Paul never did achieve any degree of success. And that blonde performer I didn't want to sign? Her name was Olivia Newton John."

For most of us, a quick review of our personal history might reveal a lengthy list of missed opportunities. Not buying stock in Coca-Cola years ago. Skipping college and getting a job instead. The great job offer you turned down. In fact, when people who were within weeks of death were quizzed about regrets, most expressed remorse over the things they didn't do rather than the things they did.

To help Christians avoid end-of-life regrets, the Lord has given us clear directives. "Have nothing to do with the fruitless deeds of darkness, but rather expose them. If you do warn the wicked person and they do not turn from their wickedness or from their evil ways, they will die for their sin; but you will have saved yourself. And do not forget to do good and to share with others, for with such sacrifices God is pleased." (Eph. 5:11; Eze. 3:19; Heb. 13:16) Be light in a dark world. Lovingly tell people how to be saved from sin. Help others.

A cartoonist wryly noted, "Google Earth gives you the opportunity to go and see anywhere in the world... so what do you do? You go and look at your house." Look beyond your house. Seize the opportunities to make both an immediate and an eternal impact on someone's life, for as Harriet Beecher Stowe wrote, "The bitterest tears shed over graves are for words left unsaid and deeds left undone."

My most significant takeaways:

How I will apply this:

Other related scriptures:

68

Getting Relationships
Eggs-actly Right

Imagine trying to drive from Niagara Falls to the Grand Canyon, navigating only with a broken GPS and a map from the early 1800's. Then imagine traversing through life's relationships using skills that are just as damaged or outdated.

How do you get relationships exactly right? The answer just might lie in eggs.

Perhaps you are always fried. If you dress daily in anger and agitation, people will avoid you like snowmen avoid south Florida beaches. Your ongoing outbursts can leave you as an outcast, even with those who care the most for you.

Maybe you are more of the deviled-egg type – plotting, scheming, and manipulating people with a devilish, self-centered approach to everything. If you treat people like puppets on a string, very soon they will cut the cord that ties them to you.

Would hard-boiled be the way some describe you? Unfortunately, when thinking of the best people skills, being hard-nosed and hard-headed doesn't typically make the list of Top Ten Traits.

Walking daily with Christ should result in a sunny-side up approach to life. Galatians 5:22-23 gives us the perfect recipe: "The fruit of the

Spirit is love, joy, peace, patience, kindness, goodness, faith, gentleness, self-control. Against such things there is no law." Wow! It's legal to be happy!

Granted, your life, like everyone else's, will have some eggs that are broken and some that are rotten. It happens. When you still choose to demonstrate the fruits of the Spirit with a sunny-side up outlook, people invariably want to find out what is bringing you such great joy. Then you can tell them about Jesus.

Making the trip through life is easier when you have the right tools. Relationships can range from challenging to cheerful, but with God's assistance, you really can get it eggs-actly right.

My most significant takeaways:

How I will apply this:

Other related scriptures:

69

Clearing the Clouds of Confusion

It was a hot summer evening in San Antonio, Texas, and Lynn and I were sitting outside with some friends at a fast-food restaurant. As much fun as we had already experienced, the highlight was yet to come. The speaker at the drive-through ordering station was extremely loud, so we easily heard this conversation:

Customer: Do you have coffee?
Server: Uh, yeah.
Customer: What is the difference between the large and the small?
Server: Uh, uh, (long pause) uh, the large, the large is bigger than the small.
Customer: (Confused silence)

Confusion creates challenges. Children become confused when their parents punish them for lying, yet tell the child to answer the phone and say their parents aren't home. Society gets confused when church leaders who preach the Ten Commandments are later discovered stealing church funds. A gentleman named Quincy Collins shared a great story that illustrates how confused some people are. He said, "Our church had finally decided to invest in a P.A. system. As the technician and I made our way around the sanctuary, we studied the best locations for the speakers. When we got to the front, the technician made a bee-line for the large opening in the front wall. He leaned over, practically disappearing. I could hear his question echoing from the baptistery, "What's a bathtub doing in a church?"'

There is no confusion where God is concerned. He speaks boldly and lovingly. His words of clarity and comfort flow freely to guide His children. When it comes to sins, the modern world attempts to convince us "the large, the large is bigger than the small." The Lord, though, has spoken His directive concerning all our shortcomings: If we confess our sins, He is faithful and righteous to forgive us our sins and to cleanse us from all unrighteousness. (1 John 1:9 HCSB)

Some things really are confusing, such as, what was the best thing before sliced bread? When it comes to getting right with God, there is nothing but certainty: Repent. Ask for forgiveness. Begin your new, purposed life walking with Him.

My most significant takeaways:

How I will apply this:

Other related scriptures:

70

Between Life and Death

Want to totally shut down casual discussion at a holiday or social gathering? Start talking about death. Most people hate the topic. Dialogue about the dark shadow stirs discomfort. Still, death sometimes does come up in conversation.

Lonnie is a man who doesn't like to be alone. In fact, he absolutely hates staying by himself when his wife, Cindy, goes out of town. Recognizing how strong that dislike is, Cindy told him, "When I die, you will probably bring a date to my funeral."

Jay Badry, former pastor and now Director of Development for Golden Gate Seminary, was most surprised when his wife unexpectedly broached the subject of death. She told Jay, "When I die, I want to be cremated." He said, "Darling, we don't need to talk about that now." "Jay," she insisted, "when I die, I want to be cremated. Then I want you to take my ashes and mix them in a gallon of paint." She smiled mischievously before continuing, "After that, I want you to use that gallon of paint to paint our bedroom ceiling!"

Philip II, King of Macedon and father of Alexander the Great, commissioned a servant to come into his presence daily and solemnly announce, "Remember, Philip, thou must die." While I wouldn't necessarily recommend having your spouse or co-worker somberly remind you "Thou must die," understanding and embracing our inevitable fate can be useful. Our clock is ticking...faster, faster, faster. What will you do with your remaining time? Serve yourself? Serve man? Serve God? Ephesians 5:15-17 (ESV) might make your decision easier: "Look carefully then how you walk, not as unwise but as wise, making the best use of the time... do not be foolish, but understand what the will of the Lord is."

One day Saint Francis was hoeing in his garden when a friend said, "What would you do if you knew you would die at sunset?" He replied, "I would finish hoeing my garden." Death is coming for all of us, even if we don't want to discuss it. Our Lord's expectation is each of us will accomplish His will – our tasks – in our assigned garden. Joseph in Egypt. Shadrach, Meshach, and Abednego in the fiery furnace. Jesus on Calvary.

It's time for me to get back to hoeing my garden. I must tell others about life.

My most significant takeaways:

How I will apply this:

Other related scriptures:

71

Great Expectations

Rev. David Taft and his wife, Lynne, were attending a funeral when, right in the middle of the very somber service, she broke into a distraught, full-blown, boo-hooing session that opened her hydrants and sent a flood of tears cascading down her face. David lovingly attempted to console (and quiet) her and asked, "Honey, what's wrong?" Through her tears she responded, "It just occurred to me that when I die, I don't know who is going to preach my funeral."

David softly said, "Darling, I will preach your funeral." There was no possible way he could have anticipated her comeback, so he just sat there dumbfounded and speechless when she said,

"You should be so broken up over my death that you couldn't preach it!"

Like it or not, expectations are a part of everyone's life. Pamela Anderson once commented, "It's great to be a blonde. With low expectations it's very easy to surprise people." Pamela might be able to manage by just meeting low expectations, but in marriages, expectations tend to run higher – much higher, and fireworks can erupt when those expectations are unmet. Dr. Bill McRae noted, "When expectations are poorly managed,...negative emotions emerge...which can be destructive in any relationship."

God's Great Marriage Manual lays out several relationship-saving tips, beginning with, "Wives, submit to your husbands in a way that is appropriate in the Lord. Husbands, love your wives and don't be harsh with them." (Colossians 3:18-19 CEB) What great advice! Applying that on a consistent basis could be the perfect medicine to improve expectations in ailing marriages.

A Kentucky mountaineer fighting overseas in WW1 kept getting nagging letters from his wife back home. He was too busy fighting to write letters, even to his wife. At last, angered by his wife's scolding letters, he sat down and wrote her: "Dear Nancy: I been a-gittin yore naggin letters all along. Now I want to tell ye, I'm tired of them. For the first time in my life I'm a-fightin in a big war, and I want to enjoy it in peace as long as it lasts."

My most significant takeaways:

How I will apply this:

Other related scriptures:

72

Avoiding That Sinking Feeling

Jim Dye absolutely, totally, loved fishing. Calling it a hobby was a disservice to his compulsion to chase the elusive bass or crappie or anything that hung out in the watery depths. As much as he delighted in fishing, Jim had a small problem. He didn't own a boat.

When you don't know what you don't know, where do you turn for guidance? To the experts, of course, and that is exactly what Jim did. He excitedly told a former co-worker and over-the-top fisherman of his newly-formed plan to step up into the big leagues by purchasing his first boat.

Jim enthusiastically asked, "What will $500 get me?"

A brief pause and a sigh preceded his friend's subdued response:

"Five hundred dollars will get you stranded in the middle of the lake."

Commitment is the key to achieving extraordinary results in virtually any endeavor. Something less will get you stranded in the middle of the lake of mediocrity.

God's Holy Word gives us amazing instruction and encouragement about commitment in our faith. The psalmist writes, "Commit your way to the Lord" (37:5). In case someone wonders exactly what that looks like, God thoughtfully tossed in very specific guidance.

The Israelites were preparing to enter the Promised Land, so Moses clearly and boldly detailed the commitment that would be required on their part: "You shall love the LORD your God with all your heart and with all your soul and with all your might" (Deut. 6:5 ESV).

All your heart. All your soul. All your might. Commitment to God above anyone or anything. That is what He asks of us.

When Jesus told Peter to step out of the boat and walk across the water to Him, the Messiah was really asking, "Are you committed to me?" This hard-charging apostle truly had unwavering dedication to his Lord. At least, he thought he did. When Peter took those first strides across the Sea of Galilee, his fear overcame his faith, and he began to sink.

Immediately after the Last Supper, Peter brashly and steadfastly proclaimed he was ready to die with Jesus. On that very same night, fear began to hammer away at Peter, and his wall of resolve crumbled like a seaside sandcastle. Just scant hours after vowing to die with Jesus, three times he denied even knowing the Master.

When Peter experienced that sinking feeling after leaving the boat, Christ reached out His hand and saved His disciple. Likewise, Jesus has made a commitment to save any and all who believe in Him: "I give them eternal life, and they will never perish, and no one will snatch them out of my hand (John 10:28 ESV).

Avoid the lake of mediocrity in your walk with God. Commit all your heart and all your soul and all your might to the Lord. Be assured, you will never sink. Never be stranded. Never perish.

Because God has committed His love to you.

My most significant takeaways:

How I will apply this:

Other related scriptures:

73

Just Let It Go

Steve Jones had a special date with his six-year-old granddaughter, Hayden. They were going to watch the movie, "Frozen." It is a movie she had seen at least forty times. A movie whose songs she had memorized. In fact, she was standing in front of the television and echoing the characters' lines as the movie began.

Since he couldn't see through his budding actress/granddaughter, Steve said, "Hayden, if I am going to watch this with you, you are going to have to move."

Hayden turned around, and with arms outstretched at her sides in exasperation, said, "Pepaw, just let it go!"

You probably have heard something similar. The words were different but the intent was the same. "Forgive and forget" is just another way of saying, "Just let it go." But those three small words pose a huge challenge. Forgiveness can be one of the hardest journeys you ever embark upon. That is, provided you even want to go down that road. A friend of mine has repeatedly said, "God will have to forgive them. I don't think I have it in me to do it."

Forgiving can be downright hard. Alternatives can be particularly enticing. Almost anything other than forgiving seems better. Revenge can be very, very appealing to us. No one likes to lose. Payback offers what seems to be a delightful, sweet, glorious chance to at least even the score.

God hears our thoughts and says, "I don't think so." He has called His followers to take the high road, even if the climb getting there is difficult. The instructions are specific. They might leave us grumbling under our breath, but the steps are clearly outlined. "Let all bitterness and wrath and anger and clamor and slander be put away from you, along with all malice." (Ephesians 4:31, ESV)

Dropping bitterness and its burdensome pals into the dumpster isn't the end of the process, though. Forgiveness of others should follow immediately. We are motivated to forgive because of Christ's example. "Be kind to one another," Paul says, "tenderhearted, forgiving one another, as God in Christ forgave you." (Ephesians 4:32 ESV)

She didn't know it, but little Hayden was delivering powerful theological wisdom. Follow her admonition. Choose the phrase that suits you best, but the meaning is the same. Just let it go. Forgive and forget. Forgive one another, as God in Christ forgave you. The words aren't necessarily important. The outcome is.

My most significant takeaways:

How I will apply this:

Other related scriptures:

74

Protecting His People

He was young, brash, and somewhat cocky. At nineteen, he didn't know what he didn't know, so when he was introduced to the world of motorcycles, advice and instruction from more seasoned riders was heard but not necessarily heeded.

Some friends took him to an abandoned mining area in central Georgia and gave him a cursory tour of a few trails before leaving him to explore the area alone. Everything went perfectly fine for the novice biker until he tackled a steep incline. Because of inexperience, he failed to downshift as the bike roared up the grade, causing the engine to sputter and die. He and the motorcycle rolled to a stop just as he reached the crest of the hill – and looked sixty feet straight down to the bottom of the mining pit.

Words fail to describe the wave of fear I felt at the moment. My self-assuredness suddenly vanished. The sickening thought that I was mere inches from performing an Evil Knievel-like launch into open space caused my entire body to tremor uncontrollably for several minutes.

It has been said, "There are only two kinds of motorcycle riders: those who've wrecked and those who are going to." God was watching over me – closely! – as He guarded my life that day. While the launch might have been majestic, the landing probably would have been messy.

Isaiah 41:10 comforts us with the words, "Do not fear, for I am with you; do not be afraid, for I am your God. I will strengthen you; I will help you; I will hold on to you with My righteous right hand." Thankfully, God helped me and held me with His right hand.

Jim Croce sang the famous cautionary words, "You don't step on Superman's cape; you don't spit into the wind." Trusting in the Lord's protection is not an invitation to live dangerously and foolishly. Life comes with warning labels God wants us to heed. After all, as the sign cautioned, "Swimming With Alligators Could Be Hazardous to Your Health!"

My most significant takeaways:

How I will apply this:

Other related scriptures:

75

The Road Home

The captivating print titled "The Road Home" features a dirt road neatly slicing through an idyllic country farm, with a barbed-wire fence on the left framing the edge of the open fields. On the right was home. The large country house, shady porch, and traditional red barn made the cozy scenario feel complete.

Something inexplicable draws us home. Familiar faces and places are like comfort food for the heart as they warmly stir delicious memories and deliver a sense of well-being. On some occasions, though, the trip home is accompanied by concerns and unease. A troubling uncertainty runs alongside our dirt road.

Tony was dying of AIDS, the sad consequence of his former homosexual lifestyle in California. Claiming Christ as his Savior had broken the chains and freed him from the way of life, but not the death sentence he carried. Going home again was necessary before journeying to his eternal home.

Tony told Greg Cox, the leader of the AIDS Care ministry team at his Nashville church, about the trip. He took the road home to New York to see his parents one last time and attempted to restore their broken relationship. "They kicked me out," he softly said. Greg kindly asked, "Couldn't they forgive you for having been homosexual?" "Oh, it wasn't that," Tony replied. "They accepted that years ago." Somewhat puzzled, Greg asked. "Then why did they kick you out?"

"They kicked me out because they couldn't accept that I am a Christian."

In 2 Timothy 3:12, Paul writes to the young apostle, "Indeed, all who desire to live a godly life in Christ Jesus will be persecuted." Get ready. It's coming. Persecution rather than pleasantries. Tony's road home led to an icy response rather than an offer to have iced tea on the shady porch.

The road home – the one leading to heaven – is the only road that truly matters. Why? Psalm 27:10 answers that question with comfort and clarity.

For my father and my mother have forsaken me, but the Lord will take me in.

My most significant takeaways:

How I will apply this:

Other related scriptures:

76

A Step in the Right Direction

Psychologist and comedian Charles Lowery, in his book, Comic Belief, shared a memorable story with a moral we need to keep in mind:

I heard about a knight who came in to see his king after a great battle. He rode in on his limping horse, leaning to one side, bloody, bruised, and scarred with his armor dented and helmet skewed. The king said, "What hath befallen you, Sir Knight?" Straightening up as best he could, he replied, "Oh, sire, I have been laboring in your service, robbing and burning and pillaging your enemies to the west." "You've been what?!" cried the startled nobleman. "I haven't any enemies to the west!" A long pause followed, and the knight finally said, "Well, Sire, you do now."

The moral to this story is enthusiasm is not enough. You need direction and a path. The question is, will you seek the right direction?

The Air Force provided my first international travel, sending me to beautiful and historic Spain. Sightseeing was a top priority when not on duty, so Lonnie Garrett and I decided to catch a train to Toledo (pronounced Toe-lay-doe), the country's oldest city. The subway got us to the area of Madrid that was somewhat near the train station. Once there, though, we were clueless as to what direction to go. I had only learned a few Spanish words and phrases during our one week in country, but we needed assistance badly. A señorita was walking nearby, so I mustered my courage and my southern-accented Spanish vocabulary. Stumbling through several halting words and phrases, I attempted to ask for directions to the train station. That sweet woman listened intently until I finally stammered out the last words. Her patient reply was fluid, easy to follow – and spoken in perfect English!

Feel lost or confused? The Lord is always ready to point us in the right direction. Do not lean on your own understanding...Call to me and I will answer you...I will teach you the way you should go; I will instruct you and advise you... The steps of a man are established by the Lord... I am the Lord your God, who leads you in the way you should go.

(Proverbs 3:5, Jeremiah 33:3, Psalm 32:8, Psalm 37:23, Isaiah 48:17)

Enthusiasm is not enough. We need direction, and God is speaking our language.

My most significant takeaways:

How I will apply this:

Other related scriptures:

77

Beware the Bison

The proprietor proudly directed my attention to the bison sculpture sitting a few feet away on the top of the showcase. Standing there with the owner, I praised the beautiful bronze piece, appreciating its exquisite detail and coloring. "Go and look at it from the other side," he suggested.

What a surprise! The opposite view revealed a Native American hunter on his pony. His right hand carried a long spear while the left supported a bison's hide that camouflaged him and his horse. His cloak of invisibility allowed the hunter to stealthily creep close to the unaware bison herd before swiftly selecting and taking down his quarry.

Of course, humans are more intelligent and observant than dumb animals – no way that we would ever be caught so easily. But 1 Corinthians 10:11-12 (The Message) cautions us, "Don't be so naive and self-confident. You're not exempt." When pompous pride comes up, our guard drops down. Like a trained assassin, sin disguises itself in order to silently slink right up beside us. You know some of the masquerades: "Everyone is doing it." "What could it hurt?" "No one will ever know." "God wants you to be happy."

Jesus advised his apostles, saying, "Watch and pray that you may not enter into temptation. The spirit indeed is willing, but the flesh is weak." (Matthew 26:41 ESV) Watch. Pray. Be alert. Satan started working to destroy lives back in the Garden of Eden, and he is still at work today.

Constant vigilance is required – thing are not always as they appear. Otherwise, like the bison, we can get separated from God and the safety and protection only He can provide.

The bottom line: Faithfully follow the Father's instructions. Listen only to His voice.

Don't get buffaloed by the wrong things.

My most significant takeaways:

How I will apply this:

Other related scriptures:

78

Honest Evaluations

Young Henry was on one of the local youth soccer teams, but at that stage, his areas of giftedness apparently did not extend to the soccer field. Let's just say he wasn't ready for the World Cup. His grandfather, a former college soccer player, offered to spend some time coaching Henry. Lots of instruction and encouragement went into the session in an effort to expand the lad's skill set, but the results were less than spectacular. Grandpa recently described the outcome to me, saying, "Henry was awful. He was just plain awful!"

On the ride home from the practice field, everyone was quiet. After a few minutes, Henry broke the silence with a most unexpected evaluation of the day, saying, "I think that went rather well, wouldn't you agree?"

Imagine Christopher Columbus, when he landed in the Bahamas instead of his intended destination of Asia, saying, "I think that went rather well!" While our self-assessments are extremely generous sometimes, thankfully we are more realistic and honest at other times.

Several years ago, Chicago Cubs relief pitcher Bob Patterson described one of his pitches, which the Cincinnati Reds' Barry Larkin hit for a game-winning home run: "It was a cross between a screwball and a change-up. It was a screw-up."

Lamentations 3:40 (The Message Bible) gives us a plain but powerful translation: Let's take a good look at the way we're living and reorder our lives under God.

Maybe it is time for an honest self-evaluation on a simple topic: How are you treating others? With dignity and respect or with disdain and resentment? Are your words and actions building relationships or building walls? Do you speak more kindly to strangers than you do to your family members, friends, and co-workers?

God has shown us how to treat others. Forgiveness is part of that formula, as are patience, understanding, compassion, and love.

Henry might have been in denial about his skills, but denying facts doesn't make them disappear. Reorder your life under God, and you will be amazed at how much your approach to people and how you deal with them improves.

My most significant takeaways:

How I will apply this:

Other related scriptures:

79

Moving Beyond
Disappointment

I was a freshman at Prichard High School in Grayson, Kentucky, and a member of the 880-Yard Relay team. After winning the regional competition on the campus of Morehead State University, we were bound for Lexington and the state track meet. For kids from a school with an enrollment of about 1,200 students in grades one through twelve, this was a really big deal. Sort of like the movie, "Hoosiers," but with winged feet instead of a basketball.

I bolted from the starting blocks at the sound of the starter's gun, sprinting into the curve, holding nothing back. The baton handoff to Tim Sayre went exactly as we had practiced hundreds of times, and he blistered down the back straightaway and around the second turn. The crowd was on its feet, roaring with excitement and encouragement. We were in third place with our two fastest runners waiting!

Larry Salley eagerly waited for Tim's command of "Go!" – and never heard it.

The crowd noise drowned out Tim, and the seamless passing of the baton never happened. Instantly, our team dropped from third place to sixth. There would be no Hoosiers-like ending for the underdogs from PHS, no gold medals draped around our necks.

Disappointment sometimes marches through your front door and makes itself at home. The marriage fails. Jobs are lost. Friendships end bitterly. Disease arrives and loved ones depart. Your grandest expectations and anticipations are suddenly derailed. How do you cope? Where do you turn?

Psalm 42:11 offers words of comfort for such disheartening moments: "Why am I so depressed? Why this turmoil within me? Put your hope in God, for I will still praise Him, my Savior and my God."

Depending on God during those dark moments helps us realize our plans are not His plans. Delight in Him always beats disappointment in life. Praising and trusting our creator tops the turmoil we feel.

"Put your hope in God." Do that, and you will always be a winner.

My most significant takeaways:

How I will apply this:

Other related scriptures:

80

The Visitors to Your Life

The month of April in Talladega, Alabama, brings a virtual symphony of color with the dogwood and redbud trees, azalea and forsythia bushes, and a bumper crop of freshly-bloomed flowers all contributing to the stunning visual concert. That gorgeous setting is the launch pad for the annual "April in Talladega" celebration.

Part of the festivities includes a tour of historic homes in what is known as the "Silk Stocking District." Lynn and I explored some of the extraordinary houses, chatting with Boyd, the owner of one of the showpieces. His face bore a combination of excitement and exhaustion. Boyd's wife had volunteered their circa 1912 home to be included in the 2015 tour. She had the easier job. His assigned role was to spend the next twelve months preparing the house for the big event. Now their perfectly-renovated residence looked like it was ready to be featured in Southern Living magazine.

But what if we had shown up eleven months earlier and asked for a tour? What dirt and disrepair would have been on display? Would an embarrassed Boyd have turned us away, telling us to come back later when everything was in order?

Our personal lives are much like the tour homes. Given enough time, we can clean up the messes and hide the unpleasant things. Jesus is far more concerned about our day-to-day presentation for those moments when someone unexpectedly walks into our life. Would our unannounced visitors be delighted or dismayed?

Visitors have a certain expectation of language, behavior, and even your attitude when the title on your personal mailbox reads, "Christian." Our Savior has an expectation as well. We are told in 1 Peter 1:15 (HCSB), "But as the One who called you is holy, you also are to be holy in all your conduct." In other words, our daily existence should be visitor-ready.

Let the Holy Spirit become the general contractor of your life. Apply a fresh coat of patience to your spirit. Plant seeds of goodness around all your interactions. Furnish your heart with love, joy, and peace. See the world through new windows of gentleness.

Allow God to make these changes and upgrades, and no one will be shocked – or disappointed – when they pull into your driveway.

My most significant takeaways:

How I will apply this:

Other related scriptures:

81

Blessing, Not Blaming

Norris Randall towered above the men at the Nashville Rescue Mission Bible study. His commanding presence and deep baritone voice captivated everyone's attention. "I've been in jail," he began. "I was jailed when I was guilty, and I was jailed when I was innocent." This story was certainly different. The audience, comprised of men who have fought some of life's hardest battles, expected truth. Norris' brutal honesty was refreshing and riveting.

"I was arrested for writing bad checks, but I was innocent. Someone had stolen my checkbook years before and now was writing bad checks. But I was the one arrested. I was in jail, but God was at work. For some reason I did not understand, I was not made to change into jail clothing. I wore my own clothes the whole time I was in there. For some reason I did not understand, my cell was never locked. I could walk in and out at will, going back and forth to other cells, talking to the men who were locked up. That was when I met a young man named Eric Goode."

Norris continued, "Eric's troubles were real. Crime, locked in jail, no money, no future. And he blamed it all on his father, who had walked out many years earlier. Eric spoke fondly of his five-year-old daughter, but he soon returned to blaming his absentee father for his woes. Norris' voice softened as he told the audience the question he posed to his angry cellmate, the question that shook the young father to his very core: "Eric, aren't you doing the same thing to your daughter?"

Norris Randall could have been angry about his situation, but God was working through him. Falsely accused. Jailed, but innocent. Locked up, but mysteriously free to move about. In street clothes, Norris looked more like a chaplain than a prisoner. God was at work. Norris told Eric about a loving Father who is always there, about a fresh start available only through Jesus. A changed life and future was available – if Eric wanted it. As Norris left him, Eric Goode quietly asked, "Mr. Norris, will you pray for me?"

"Do not do wrong to repay a wrong…repay with a blessing, because you yourselves were called to do this so that you might receive a blessing." (1 Peter 3:9 NCV)

My most significant takeaways:

How I will apply this:

Other related scriptures:

82

Holding On or Turning Loose

Moving from one home to another has reminded me of a great truth: we hold on to things we should let go of. Items that have not seen the light of day for twenty years are rediscovered. Objects we call cherished keepsakes reemerge from hiding, although slightly more rusted or mildewed than when we last saw them. Granted, not everything should be tossed aside. The very real opposite is we sometimes hold onto things that should be turned over to someone else.

Matt Moore was at the Opryland USA theme park several years ago and had excitedly settled into his seat on the Hangman roller coaster. The teen-aged ride operator began the mandatory safety warning announcement, his boredom with the repetitive process evidenced by his lifeless delivery: "Be sure to remove or secure all hats, sunglasses, purses, bags, umbrellas, or any other items that could come loose during the ride." The young man was jolted from the routineness of his job when one young lady said, "Wait a second," reached down below her seat, and then said "Hold this please" as she raised up and handed him her prosthetic leg!

People tend to collect things. A high school classmate, Jerri Lynn Shaffer, told me her mother kept milk cartons - hundreds and hundreds of milk cartons. Jerri Lynn finally asked, "Momma, why do you have so many milk cartons?" Her mother answered, "I use them to water my dog." "Momma!" Jerri Lynn exclaimed, "You only have one dog!"

You might gather recipe books, antiques, or arrowheads. For others it might be fishing lures, carnival glass, or Civil War relics. These occupy space in your home, but they aren't harmful. On the other hand, if you have collected grudges, insults, rejections, and painful memories for decades, trouble lies ahead. Anger and hatred are the main ingredients of a recipe for disaster. Perhaps it is time to turn loose. Ephesians 4:26, 27, 31 (NIV) guides us in saying, "In your anger do not sin... and do not give the devil a foothold. Get rid of all bitterness, rage and anger, brawling and slander, along with every form of malice."

The move into our new home has prompted us to turn loose of things we needed to let go of. Turn your harsh, hurtful feelings over to the operator of the universe. You will discover your ride through life will much more enjoyable.

My most significant takeaways:

How I will apply this:

Other related scriptures:

83

No Other Way

Almost everyone has seen something they want…maybe even something they REALLY, REALLY want. Such was the situation with thirteen-year-old Gunnar, who had been introduced to handling and using guns by his grandfather, Danny Waggoner. In fact, one of Danny's guns had become Gunnar's personal favorite, to the point that he deeply coveted the firearm. Not known for his subtlety, one of his very frequent sayings became, "I think I should inherit that gun."

One day Gunnar was with Grandma Judy and his aunt Mindy, and the topic of discussion happened to be Danny's guns. Never one to miss an opportunity, Gunnar repeated what had become his mantra, "I think I should inherit that gun. I think I should inherit that gun." It suddenly occurred to Judy and Mindy that Gunnar probably did not really know what "inherit" meant, let alone fully comprehend the most important factor associated with "inherit." Mindy pulled him to her and gently shared, "Gunnar, in order for you to inherit Papaw Danny's gun, Papaw Danny would have to die."

Disbelief. Uncertainty. Then Gunnar's look of confusion quickly turned to one of clarity. He immediately went to his grandfather, gave him a big, loving hug and said, "Papaw Danny, I don't want you to die. But I sure do want that gun!"

Jesus' disciples experienced a similar dilemma when the Lord told them what was about to occur: "From that time on Jesus began to explain to his disciples that he must go to Jerusalem and suffer many things at the hands of the elders, the chief priests and the teachers of the law, and that he must be killed and on the third day be raised to life." (Matthew 16:21 NIV) His followers felt sick. Denial reigned. If God's Son could cast out demons, surely He could cast aside any physical threat. Peter shot back, "Never, Lord!" he said. "This shall never happen to you!" (v. 22)

The disciples couldn't buy it. They wanted to sit at His right hand, not in a receiving line at a funeral home. His devoted supporters envisioned being in His kingdom, not being at the foot of His cross. "I don't want you to die!"

Aren't we like Gunnar, like the disciples? We want what we want. Salvation. Forgiveness. Undeserved mercy. We just expect that there has to be some way around the price of eternal death.

And we are wrong. There is no other way.

Jesus, I didn't want you to die. But I am thankful that you did – for me.

My most significant takeaways:

How I will apply this:

Other related scriptures:

84

Appearances Can Be Deceiving

Ron Shearin was working for NASA on the Apollo space program in the 1960's, and the first launch following his employment was scheduled soon. He and his wife, Roma, were excited that she could witness the launch live. Historic moments like that should be captured with photographs, but the Shearins didn't own a nice camera. The night before the launch, they bought a used Minolta 35mm camera with multiple lenses and accessories. Unfortunately, they didn't have time to purchase a quality camera case, so Roma put everything into a brown paper bag.

On the shuttle ride to the observation point, Roma was seated beside a gentleman who held a gorgeous, professional-looking camera case. She felt a bit embarrassed by her brown paper bag, but it would have to do for the day.

They settled into their seats upon arrival, and the man ceremoniously opened his case and pulled out...a Kodak Instamatic camera! Meanwhile, Roma noisily unrolled the top of the brown paper bag and took out her sophisticated, single-lens-reflex camera. She quickly replaced the normal-view lens with a long telephoto lens, mounted the camera to a shoulder brace, and hoisted it into position.

The gentleman's mouth hung open in astonishment. "Where did you learn to do that?" he asked incredulously. "My husband taught me," Roma responded, "last night."

Perhaps you have experienced despondent moments when you felt like a brown paper bag surrounded by beautiful and professional people. Guess what? God made you, and God isn't concerned about your looks. 1 Samuel 16:7 clearly states that God knows looks can be deceiving: "The Lord sees not as man sees: man looks on the outward appearance, but the Lord looks on the heart."

Our Father wants to know if our heart is right, filled with love and compassion and a genuine repentance of our wrongdoings. Handsome or pretty, dressed in fine clothes, attending church religiously – those things do not concern God.

He simply wants to know one thing – what is inside your brown paper bag?

My most significant takeaways:

How I will apply this:

Other related scriptures:

85

Step Up To the Plate

Our waitress, "Angie," impressively approached us with our orders. She deftly dodged other patrons while skillfully balancing seven full-sized breakfasts – four on one arm and three on the other. Angie was inspiring! She was light on her feet! She was a picture of grace and confidence! And she was almost successful.

Just as Angie reached our table, her load shifted slightly, starting a chain reaction of crashing plates that was reminiscent of one of Dick Van Dyke's slapstick routines. Potatoes and pancakes sailed across the restaurant as she vainly attempted to corral the runaway breakfasts. To her credit, she did manage to trap one plate under her left armpit. Doing her best to reestablish a sense of decorum, Angie pulled out the lone surviving meal, held it up, and calmly asked, "Okay, who had ham and eggs?"

Most of us have experienced periods where excesses threatened to upset the precarious balance we strive so hard to maintain. The loads, tasks, and demands are ever-increasing. Whether the blocks on your wagon are labeled church or children, special projects or spouse, work or weekend warrior, the load can get out of control. Your life starts to feel like the performer on the old variety show who began by spinning one plate on a tiny pole. He added a second plate and pole, running back to spin the first plate again. More plates and poles were added until he reached his known limit and kept all spinning...or until he pushed the boundaries too far and then watched helplessly as his show became a sad spectacle.

Let's begin by agreeing that God does not want us to be a one-man show. His directive, "Bear one another's burdens." (Galatians 6:2 ESV), means we are not only to assist but we are to allow others to lighten our load. Jehovah Himself is prepared to step if people will just push aside their pride and ask for help. The Lord says, "Come to me, all who labor and are heavy laden, and I will give you rest." (Matthew 11:28 ESV)

The mess Angie was responsible for looked like the aftermath of a middle-school food fight. Her morning would have been much calmer (and cleaner!) if she had just requested help, even momentarily. Give up the juggling act. Trust God. Ask God. He is ready and waiting to lovingly help you when you have too much on your plate.

My most significant takeaways:

How I will apply this:

Other related scriptures:

86

The Temptations

One of the best-kept secrets of San Antonio is a restaurant called the Magic Time Machine. It is a fun setting where servers dress up as cartoon characters, movie stars, superheroes, or pop culture icons. Several years ago my wife and I were there with a group of men from my military class at Lackland Air Force Base. While King Arthur and Sir Lancelot were our servers for the delightful meal, another experience awaited the men in our group at the end of our visit.

Just as we prepared to leave, the Playboy Bunny appeared at our table in her skimpy Bunny attire. Her job: to sit on each man's lap and feed him grapes. Lynn and I have differing recollections at this point in the story. It seems to me the lady was skinny and rather unattractive. Lynn says she was beautiful and rather curvaceous and well-endowed. At any rate, the Bunny started at the opposite end of our semi-circle table, snuggling into each man's lap and tantalizingly feeding him fresh grapes. Eventually the moment arrived where I was the only man left.

As the Bunny started toward me, Lynn stared at her and spoke in even, measured tones as she coolly said, "If you touch him, you die."

The Bunny instantly froze mid-stride, nervously looking at Lynn and then back at me. Looked again at Lynn and back at me. Fear paralyzed her. What to do? Her self-preservation instinct kicked in. She eyed the distance between us, stretched out her arm as far as she could reach, and cautiously inched just close enough to feed me a single, forlorn grape.

The lures of life abound, and everyone is a target. "No temptation has overtaken you that is not common to man. Each person is tempted when he is lured and enticed by his own desire." (1 Cor. 10:13; James 1:14 ESV) Dining out or driving around. At work or out for a walk. Satan sows sin nuggets as prolifically as Johnny Appleseed sowed apple seeds in frontier territories. When Jesus' disciples asked Him to teach them to pray, part of the model prayer the Lord shared with them was "And lead us not into temptation, but deliver us from evil." (Matthew 6:13) Jesus knew we needed lots of help to resist temptation.

Be thankful that someone stands in the gap when the temptations threaten you. God has placed that person there at the precise moment you need them most.

(And I still say she was skinny.)

My most significant takeaways:

How I will apply this:

Other related scriptures:

87

A Kaleidoscope of Christmas Perspectives

If you are still working on your personal Christmas wish list of "stuff" you want, Jesus offers this suggestion: "But seek first the kingdom of God and His righteousness, and all these things will be provided for you." (Matthew 6:33)

G. K. Chesterton was a British writer and Christian apologist. He wrote, "When we were children we were grateful to those who filled our stockings at Christmas time. Why are we not grateful to God for filling our stockings with legs?"

Author Andy Andrews noted, "When our youngest son was seven, he asked, 'If tomorrow's Christmas Eve, is today Christmas Adam?' And it has been so ever since!"

Emily Reasonover is a Hermitage stay-at-home mother with a special needs child named Lee. She posted on Facebook: Lee just asked the cutest thing. "Mommy, does Santa have a wife?" I said, "Yes, Mrs. Claus is his wife." Lee replied, "I thought Mary Christmas was his wife."

Writer Andy Rooney, a fixture on the CBS show 60 Minutes for 33 years, offered a delightful approach to Christmas: "One of the most glorious messes in the world is the mess created in the living room on Christmas day. Don't clean it up too quickly."

Comedian Bob Hope took Jesus' words to heart when he said, "My idea of Christmas, whether old-fashioned or modern, is very simple: loving others. Come to think of it, why do we have to wait for Christmas to do that?"

"Christmas is not a time nor a season, but a state of mind. To cherish peace and goodwill, to be plenteous in mercy, is to have the real spirit of Christmas." – President Calvin Coolidge

Newspaper columnist George Matthew Adams correctly observed, "The birth of the baby Jesus stands as the most significant event in all history, because it has meant the pouring into a sick world of the healing medicine of love which has transformed all manner of hearts for almost two thousand years."

Adopt the perspective of Christmas for what it was meant to be: the greatest of gifts to the most unworthy recipients. Be grateful. Share the gift of God's love with others so they, too, can receive the Lord's compassion and caring.

Merry Christmas!

My most significant takeaways:

How I will apply this:

Other related scriptures:

88

See You At the Pole

Jonathan, Christopher, and Alina were spending the night with us so their parents, Jeff and Barbara Shirley, could enjoy a well-deserved night out. The next morning, Lynn caught Jonathan, their oldest son, attempting to kick her dog (not a good move on his part). She immediately warned Jonathan, but soon his temptation became too great. Though his second kick also missed the target, it was not missed by Lynn's watchful eye. She immediately marched Jonathan to a corner and made him stand there with his nose against the wall. His punishment of several minutes was rather severe since he was a hyper-active child, and it was made even worse since Christopher and Alina witnessed his penalty.

His parents were rather impressed with the effectiveness of Lynn's action, so when Jonathan misbehaved just a few nights later at K-Mart, Jeff and Barbara made him stand with his nose against a nearby pole. Little Alina wasn't quite sure what to do when she saw her big brother standing there alone and embarrassed in his public humiliation, so she timidly walked to the pole, placed her tiny nose against it, and stood there with Jonathan in a show of compassionate support.

It is easy to gruffly adopt a hands-off attitude that says, "He brought this on himself" when someone messes up. After all, should you be put out because of someone else's thoughtlessness, selfishness, or inconsiderate actions? God's answer to that question is a definitive "Yes." Galatians 6:2 (HCSB) instructs us to "Carry one another's burdens." Jesus carried our burden of sin and shame and modeled how we should conduct ourselves in His name. If we add to that 1 John 4:21, which reads, "We have this command from Him: The one who loves God must also love his brother," we will be like Alina and head for our brother's pole.

C.H.Mackintosh wrote: "There is power in the presence of a risen Savior to solve our difficulties, remove our perplexities, calm our fears, ease our burdens, dry our tears, meet our every need, tranquilize our minds and satisfy every craving of our hearts." Isn't now a great time to quit kicking opportunities aside? Help lighten someone's load – look for a brother or sister to love and support in Christ's name.

See you at the pole.

My most significant takeaways:

How I will apply this:

Other related scriptures:

89

Paying the Price

The young man and woman made their way to the front of the home and asked to see Mr. Griffin. They graduated from the University of Florida only a couple of years earlier and had readily agreed to participate in fund-raising for a new hospital wing. Their assignment: encourage other Florida alumni to donate.

The fund-raisers were told Mr. Griffin was out back in the garden. As they hesitantly made their way through the muddy soil between rows of vegetables, they presented a rather comical sight. With him dressed in coat and tie and her in a skirt suit and high heels, it was reminiscent of a scene from the old Green Acres television show. In contrast, they found Mr. Griffin busily hoeing weeds while wearing bib overalls, a long-sleeved plaid shirt, and dirty brogans.

After introductions, the freshly-scrubbed young professionals told Mr. Griffin the purpose of their visit – raising money for a new hospital wing. Mr. Griffin asked, "How much will it cost?" The young man replied, "It will be three and one-half million dollars. We are looking to Florida alumni like yourself to help out if at all possible. Any amount you can contribute would be greatly appreciated." Mr. Griffin nodded, pulled a checkbook out of his sweaty overalls, and wrote a check that he folded in half and handed to the young lady. They expressed their gratitude and quickly exited, once more tiptoeing gently through the beans and corn stalks.

After driving a short distance, the young lady curiously opened the check to see how much Mr. Griffin had donated. Her mouth fell open in amazement. The man asked, "How much? How much did he give?" She mumbled, "He paid it all. Three and a half million dollars. He paid it all!"

When the opportunity to help heal and to give life was before him, Ben Hill Griffin, whom the University of Florida football stadium is named for, paid it all.

When the opportunity to help heal mankind's hurt and to give eternal life was before Him, Jesus paid it all. Greater love has no one than this, that someone lay down his life for his friends. For you were bought with a price. So glorify God in your body. (John 15:13; 1 Corinthians 6:20 ESV)

My most significant takeaways:

How I will apply this:

Other related scriptures:

90

What Really Bugs You?

Not everything in life needs to be broadcast worldwide. Most people prefer to keep some things quiet. Relationship issues. Losing a job. Even medical concerns.

Several years ago, Lloyd Stinnett moved into an apartment that apparently had not been well kept. The previous renter actually had moved away but left some of their pets behind. Their pet cockroaches. Lloyd became painfully aware of that situation when the sensation of something moving inside his ear awakened him around 2:00 a.m. He tried everything he could think of to evict this unwelcome intruder. Flushing his ear with water, drowning the pest in baby oil, chasing it around with a Q-tip – nothing at all convinced the cockroach to get out of Dodge.

Finally Lloyd went to the emergency room at Southern Hills Hospital in Nashville. As he approached the registration desk, the receptionist barked out, "How can I help you?" Lloyd whispered, "I have a cockroach in my ear." "What?" she asked. Somewhat embarrassed by the circumstances, he whispered just slightly louder, "I have a cockroach in my ear." The receptionist stared at him for a moment, turned and yelled at a co-worker on the other side of the room, "Hey, Judy, how much do we charge to get a cockroach out of a guy's ear?"

Do you have something running around in your head? God already knows: "Would not God discover this? For he knows the secrets of the heart." Psalm 44:21 (ESV) He is aware of your angry thoughts, your lustful thoughts, your greedy thoughts. He knows how the memories of past misdeeds haunt you. The Lord is fully aware of the shame and embarrassment that never leave. He knows.

Whatever is bugging you can be dealt with easily. No emergency room required. No loud receptionist between you and the Great Physician. The cure lies in a simple prescription coined in an old hymn: "Just a little talk with Jesus makes it right." The reassuring and comforting words of 1 James 1:9 promise, "If we confess our sins, he is faithful and just to forgive us our sins and to cleanse us from all unrighteousness."

Whisper your sins to God. It is a confidential matter between you and Him.

My most significant takeaways:

How I will apply this:

Other related scriptures:

91

Perfect Freedom – by Charles W. Colson

As one who has served time in prison and has since spent most of my life working in them, I'll never forget the most unusual prison I've ever visited.

Called Humaita Prison, it is in Sao Jose dos Campos in Brazil. Formerly a government prison, it is now operated by Prison Fellowship Brazil as an alternative prison, without armed guards or high-tech security. Instead, it is run on the Christian principles of love of God and respect for men.

Humaita has only two full-time staff; the rest of the work is done by the 730 inmates serving time for everything from murder and assault to robbery and drug-related crimes. Every man is assigned another inmate to whom he is accountable. In addition, each prisoner is assigned a volunteer mentor from the outside who works with him during his term and after his release. Prisoners take classes on character development and are encouraged to participate in educational and religious programs.

When I visited this prison, I found the inmates smiling – particularly the murderer who held the keys, opened the gates and let me in. Wherever I walked, I saw men at peace. I saw clean living areas.

I saw people working industriously. The walls were decorated with motivational sayings and Scripture.

Humaita has an astonishing record. Its recidivism rate is 4 percent, compared to 75 percent in the rest of Brazil. How is that possible?

I saw the answer when my inmate guide escorted me to the notorious cell once used for solitary punishment. Today, he told me, it always houses the same inmate. As we reached the end of the long concrete corridor and he put the key into the lock, he paused and asked, "Are you sure you want to go in?"

"Of course," I replied impatiently. "I've been in isolation cells all over the world." Slowly he swung open the massive door, and I saw the prisoner in that cell: a crucifix, beautifully carved – Jesus, hanging on the cross.

"He's doing time for the rest of us," my guide said softly.

(Chicken Soup for the Christian Soul, 1997, Health Communications, Deerfield Beach, Florida)

My most significant takeaways:

How I will apply this:

Other related scriptures:

92

Being Heard and Being Loved

You probably remember when your parents tended to take an authoritative, "I-know-what-is-best" approach when you wanted or needed something. That is the situation Stacy Holland found himself in during a critical moment in his young life. He was six years old, and he was the next batter in a high-stakes T-ball game. Stacy told his Dad, "I need to go to the bathroom." His father responded, "You can hold it." Stacy pleaded, "No, I really need to go." His Dad answered with a louder tone of finality when he said, "You can hold it. Now get up there and hit."

Being the obedient son and team player, Stacy dutifully did as he was told, driving the ball into the outfield. He vividly recalls running the basepaths – and leaving a wet trail in the dust from home plate all the way around to third base!

When someone truly listens to another person, they send an incredibly powerful message that can build or deepens a connection with the speaker. By not being dismissive when someone expresses a thought or shares a need, the listener communicates, "You are important to me." This principle applies whether you are listening to your spouse, a child, a neighbor, co-worker, or friend. Everyone needs another person who will truly listen to them. Sometimes we do well. And then...

On Christmas afternoon, the Pastor's wife dropped into an easy chair saying, "Boy! Am I ever tired!" Her husband looked over at her and said, "I had to conduct two special services last night, three today, and give a total of five sermons. Why are you so tired?" "Dearest," she replied, "I had to listen to all of them."

Psalm 34:15 (NIV) tells us God never tires of intently listening to his children: "The Lord sees the good people and listens to their prayers." The apostle John shares a most comforting thought when he says, "This is the confidence we have in approaching God: that if we ask anything according to his will, he hears us. And if we know that he hears us—whatever we ask—we know that we have what we asked of him." (1 John 5:14-15 NIV)

It is wonderful to know that whether we're young or old, our heavenly Father takes a time out when He hears us call. Thank you for loving and listening to us, God.

My most significant takeaways:

How I will apply this:

Other related scriptures:

93

Showing Some Love

Terry McClure was walking down the streets of Dollywood, pushing Karen, his wife, in a wheelchair. They were accompanied by their daughter-in-law and two grandchildren on this well-deserved vacation to Pigeon Forge, Tennessee. He worked hard and he worked lots of hours, and this brief getaway was sorely needed.

As they made their way down the streets of Dollywood, Terry noticed people watching him and his family. Other park visitors began to smile broadly, wave, and some even clapped. This warm outburst of love was a rather pleasant and totally unexpected surprise. Being an affable guy, Terry soaked in the adulation from both sides of the street and cheerfully returned their smiles as he enthusiastically waved with gratitude back to these appreciative tourists.

Then Terry happened to glance over his shoulder – and saw Dolly Parton coming up the street behind him!

Everyone likes to feel special, whether you are a celebrity or not. Since being loved is one of our greatest needs, a craving that doesn't diminish with age, Jesus made sure He addressed that as part of His directions for how we should live and act. John 13:34-35 quotes the Master: "A new commandment I give to you, that you love one another: just as I have loved you, you also are to love one another. By this all people will know that you are my disciples, if you have love for one another."

One act. Two benefits. That single, glistening droplet of love you pour into someone's parched life not only quenches their need, but more importantly, they (and anyone else around) get to witness first-hand one of Christ's followers being faithful to His commandment. Real Christian love – in action, not just in words.

When was the last time you surprised someone and made them feel like a music superstar? Decide to brighten up a few lives. Smile. Clap and wave. Shine a spotlight on some hard-working guys and gals by showing them some love. No special training or tools are required. You are fully prepared right now – "If you have love for one another."

My most significant takeaways:

How I will apply this:

Other related scriptures:

94

Take Notice

Quiet and relaxing. A nice, casual steak dinner. That was all David and Lisa Benton wanted for their night out. David, however, tends to be a noticer. He notices the usual and unusual people and activities alike. People studying menus. Millenials engrossed with electronics. Dinner partners who are sitting silently, together but alone. And then David noticed a frantic-looking woman bending over a gentleman who appeared to be in distress. Apparently no one else noticed.

David immediately made his way to the diner and asked if he needed help, eliciting a barely audible "Yes!" David doubted whether he could lift this rather large guy, but fortunately the patron was able to somewhat stand under his own power. David's quickly delivered a Heimlich maneuver thrust. Nothing. "It is going to have to be a lot harder," David thought. This time an emphatic drive into the man's midsection sent a bite of steak sailing across the table. Mission accomplished. A life saved.

Once the gentleman regained his composure, David returned to his table without any expectations. And he noticed something rather odd. The customer, his wife, nor any other patrons said anything. Not a single "Thank you" was shared. Customers didn't applaud. The staff never mentioned the episode. No one offered to pay for David and Lisa's dinner. Have heroics now become ho-hum, expected events?

Luke tells how Jesus was beseeched by ten lepers to have mercy on them, so He healed them. He directed them to go and show themselves to the priest, the standard practice for someone who had been cleansed. 'One of them, when he realized that he was healed, turned around and came back, shouting his gratitude. He kneeled at Jesus' feet, so grateful. He couldn't thank him enough – and he was a Samaritan. Jesus said, "Were not ten healed? Can none be found to come back and give glory to God except this outsider?"' (Luke 17:15-17 MSG)

The diner in the restaurant. Nine remaining lepers. You and me. Something incredible was done for us. We were saved when we could not save ourselves. Writer William Arthur Ward opined, "Feeling gratitude and not expressing it is like wrapping a present and not giving it." Shouldn't we give the gift of heartfelt gratitude? After all, nothing was owed. There was no requirement for someone to rescue us. David Benton noticed a man in need and saved his life. A descendant of King David noticed our need and saved us. To both, let's say, "Thank you."

My most significant takeaways:

How I will apply this:

Other related scriptures:

95

The Real Thing

For decades Coca-Cola used multiple forms of advertising to declare to the world, "It's the Real Thing." Not just speaking of a soft drink, but isn't "the real thing" what everyone wants? Substitutes often fail to measure up to our expectations. "The Real Thing" experienced a real public relations nightmare when New Coke was introduced in 1985. Football fans threw a penalty flag on the National Football League's substitute referees during the 2012 season.

Some things simply cannot be substituted for. When it comes to effective leadership or great customer service, only the real thing will do. A medical degree from a university in Liberia will not suffice if you want to provide medical care for my family. Selling fake Nike or Coach products will probably let you experience the real judicial system.

Real joy. True love. Genuine relationships. People want the real thing. We are magically drawn to authenticity. Ethical behavior and truthfulness are powerful beacons we gravitate toward. The odds are you would you never consider buying a product or service from a company that advertises, "We're the Phony Thing."

Where can we turn to escape the counterfeits that clutter our lives? God is the only unfailing source that has ever existed. When we consider lasting commitment, God qualifies. From the creation of Adam and Eve to the billions of people who inhabit earth today, God has been committed to the very best for mankind. Psalm 117:2 clearly states, "For great is his love toward us, and the faithfulness of the LORD endures forever."

The movie *Catch Me If You Can* is based on the life of Frank Abagnale, the scam artist who successfully posed as a Georgia doctor, a Louisiana parish prosecutor, and a Pan American pilot. The New Testament details the life of Jesus Christ the doctor, prosecutor, and commander of the skies. Jesus actually healed the sick; He will return as prosecutor to judge the living and the dead; and the Lord will lift His family into the clouds upon His return.

Frank Abagnale faked his roles. Jesus really lived His.

Skip the substitutes. There is nothing like the Real Thing.

My most significant takeaways:

How I will apply this:

Other related scriptures:

96

Christmas Memories

Almost everyone has distinctive Christmas memories etched into their personal recollections. Fleeting scenes as we recall a bearded seven-year-old Joseph and a blonde-haired Mary in the children's Christmas play. Enticing aromas. Christmas candy. The delight in particular gifts, or the disappointment when Santa did not deliver your most-desired item. Joyous family gatherings dominate the scrapbook for some, while others painfully recall spending the holiday alone. Perhaps you are right now flipping through the mental photo album of your Christmases past.

The great classical cellist Pablo Casals, in his life story entitled *Joys and Sorrows*, tells readers his first memory of attending worship on Christmas Eve when he was five-years-old. He walked to the church in a small village in Spain, hand-in-hand with his father, who was the church's organist.

He said that as he walked, he shivered. The shivering was not, however, so much because the night was cold, though it was quite cold. Pablo was shivering because the atmosphere that evening was so electric and so mysterious.

"I felt," Pablo said, "that something wonderful was about to happen. High overhead, the heavens were full of stars, and as we walked in silence, I held tightly to my father's hand… In the dark, narrow streets, there were moving figures, shadowy and spectral and silent, too, moving into the church, quickly and silently… My father played the organ, and when I sang, it was really my heart that was singing, and I poured out everything that was in me."

"It was really my heart that was singing." That must have been the emotional response Mary experienced when she learned she would bear God's son. She said, "Oh, how I praise the Lord. How I rejoice in God my Savior! For he took notice of his lowly servant girl, and now generation after generation forever shall call me blest of God. For he, the mighty Holy One, has done great things to me." (Luke 1:46-49 NIV)

This year, create Christmas memories around one simple phrase: "in the town of David a Savior has been born to you." Enjoy and share the splendor of the celebration of the birth of our King. Be filled with rejoicing, wonder, and thanks. Then let your heart do the singing!

My most significant takeaways:

How I will apply this:

Other related scriptures:

97

Facing the Future Fearlessly

Today's world is daunting. Troubling. Most uncertain. The winds of change swirl with gale-force intensity.

For many people, their natural resistance to change is magnified one hundred-fold as the expected and the normal are swept away by a tsunami of change. When facing an ambiguous road ahead, folks can become virtually paralyzed by fear.

A questionable future is not new to the twenty-first century. The accompanying fear was as real way back when as it is today. The Old Testament presents example after example of both individuals and groups who were hesitant to take another step forward. Fear froze them in place like ice-covered statues.

The mindset of fear and doubt is not God's plan for us. The Lord speaks to us 365 times in the Bible, reminding us again and again, "Fear not."

A classic example is presented when the Israelites were poised to step into the promised land. Moses was instructing God's chosen tribe, telling them he would not be going with them. Joshua would be assuming the leadership role. Knowing the people had a propensity to expect the worst, Moses offered reassurance. He told the people how God was going to make them victorious over the kings and armies before them.

Big changes. A big step forward. And big fears that shook their confidence. But God wasn't finished speaking through Moses: "Be strong and courageous. Do not fear or be in dread of them, for it is the LORD your God who goes with you. He will not leave you or forsake you." Deuteronomy 31:6 (ESV)

Demonstrate strength. Act courageously. Push aside your fear. Because you aren't going in alone. Words that were true then are just as true today. If the yet-to-come seems filled with ominous dread and foreboding darkness, consider this rewrite of Moses' words to be personalized just for you:

Be strong and courageous.

Do not fear or be in dread of the future,

for it is the LORD your God who goes with you.

He will not leave you or forsake you.

The future may come with overwhelming fears and anxieties. Recognize you aren't stepping into that battlefield without reinforcements. God goes with you. He will not leave you or forsake you. And that comforting assurance equips you to be, as God directed, strong and courageous. Fear not.

My most significant takeaways:

How I will apply this:

Other related scriptures:

98

The God Who Provides

"And my God will supply every need of yours according to his riches in glory in Christ Jesus." (Philippians 4:19 ESV)

Brad and his South Carolina church worked several months getting connected to west Africa. With the help of a missionary in the area, Brad and his mission team found a village they virtually adopted. What that meant was a commitment to send teams to that village for a period of time. Teams that would minister to the village. Teams that would share the gospel. Teams that would love the people. Teams that would enter a village made up of about 3,000 Muslims.

God never says all our tasks would be easy. Through the faithful efforts of the faithful Christians, ten of the local people devoted their lives to Jesus. That nucleus of ten was enough to plant a church within the village. Unlike other parts of the world (and because of God's protective oversight), the Muslims of this village were not extreme in their beliefs. They saw no reason to kill their countrymen who had left the Muslim faith. Instead, the village was very receptive to Brad and his church being there. They even gave Brad's church a small parcel of land where they could build a storage building for their equipment, saving them the effort of shipping everything back and forth each time a team came to serve.

One particular year, Brad's team was in the village during drought season. The natives are farmers. If they don't grow crops, they don't eat. If they don't eat, they starve. Because of the extended period without rain, several of the local farmers went to the Muslim Imam and said, "Would you pray to Allah that it would rain so that our crops would grow and we would have food?" The Imam listened carefully before replying, "I will do that. But I want you to know that it could take two or three years for Allah to answer our prayer."

Two years? Three years? It was a sentence of certain, slow death. Downcast and defeated, the farmers turned to leave but were stopped cold when the Imam continued, "The Christians are in the village. Go to the Christians and ask them to petition their God that it will rain, because their God always answers their prayer."

The contingency immediately found Brad and relayed the Imam's message. They pleaded. They begged. Pray. Pray for rain. Pray so our families can live. Pray.

Pressure? Eyes filled with desperation are imploring, "Call upon your God. The God the Muslim Imam said always answers prayers." No pressure, right? Brad nodded to the men. Then he prayed...expectantly. He prayed for rain. He prayed that believers and Muslims alike would have water for their crops. He prayed.

How many times have you prayed, only to discover God did not answer your prayer? Or He did not answer in your way? Or in your time frame? We want our answer. Instantly. If it is any comfort, the same God who did not give the answer you wanted also did not answer Brad's prayer. There was no immediate deluge from the skies. No gentle life-giving rain began when the prayer ended. God did not answer the prayer that afternoon. But then nightfall came. At about ten o'clock came a frog-strangling, gulley-washing rain like they had not seen in years. The God who always answers prayers did so again.

Some will read this true story and simply say, "Oh, that is nothing more than coincidence." Believe that if you like, but be assured of one thing: There are three thousand Muslims in that village who know the

Muslim god could not answer the prayer but the Christian God could. He is the God who provides.

A son for Abraham. A walkway through the Red Sea when the Israelites needed an escape route. Accuracy when the stone left David's sling. A Savior for all of mankind. Whether it was Elijah calling down fire from heaven or Brad calling for rain from heaven, God listens. He answers. And He provides.

"If you then, who are evil, know how to give good gifts to your children, how much more will your Father who is in heaven give good things to those who ask him!" (Matthew 7:11)

My most significant takeaways:

How I will apply this:

Other related scriptures:

99

Count Your Many Blessings

Americans will pause this week to give thanks. Some of our citizens will struggle with that concept. It has been a hard year for many. On top of the rocks that life typically hurls at us, a pandemic descended upon our world. The virus took loved ones. COVID robbed us of life events, jobs, and freedoms. Recalibrating routines and finances became essential. Reassessing priorities suddenly ranked at the top of everyone's To-Do list.

In the eye of the hurricane, there is peace and calm, a nugget of good surrounded by devastation. The same is true for us. Even in the midst of frightening and turbulent times, we must remember to be thankful to God.

While on a short-term mission trip, Pastor Jack Hinton was leading worship at a leper colony on the island of Tobago. A woman who had been facing away from the pulpit turned around.

"It was the most hideous face I had ever seen," Hinton said. "The woman's nose and ears were entirely gone. She lifted a fingerless hand in the air and asked, 'Can we sing "Count Your Many Blessings"?'"

Overcome with emotion, Hinton left the service. He was followed by a team member who said, "I guess you'll never be able to sing that song again."

"Yes I will," he replied, "but I'll never sing it the same way."

Today, count YOUR many blessings. And then thank the One who filled your life with those many, amazing gifts.

My most significant takeaways:

How I will apply this:

Other related scriptures:

100

The Baby Camel

(Thank you to Phil Baker for sharing this story.)

The other day I heard about a baby camel that asked, "Mom, why do I have these huge three-toed feet? The mother replied, "To help you stay on top of the soft sand while trekking across the desert."

"And why the long eyelashes?"

"To keep sand out of your eyes on our trips through the desert."

"Why the humps?"

"To store water for our long treks across the barren desert."

The baby camel considered that and then said, "That's great, Mom. We have huge feet to keep us from sinking, long eyelashes to keep sand out of our eyes, and humps to store water. But, Mom...."

"Yes, son?"

"Why are we in the zoo?"

Perhaps you have asked yourself that very question: Why am I in this zoo called life? God has emphatically answered that question for His children:

"Go, therefore, and make disciples of all nations, baptizing them in the name of the Father and of the Son and of the Holy Spirit, teaching them to observe everything I have commanded you. And remember, I am with you always, to the end of the age." (Matthew 28:19-20 HCSB)

My most significant takeaways:

How I will apply this:

Other related scriptures:

www.ingramcontent.com/pod-product-compliance
Lightning Source LLC
Chambersburg PA
CBHW060509130626
46553CB00002B/440